Praise for

THE POWER OF "MEH"

"If you've ever felt overwhelmed by your thoughts or stuck trying to fix what maybe just needs a shrug, *The Power of MEH* is for you. This fun, insightful read blends powerful mental health tools—like radical acceptance and cognitive defusion—with the freeing concept of *meh*. It's simple, effective, and surprisingly life-changing. I connected with it instantly and have already started using 'meh' as a personal mantra—and honestly, it works! If you're ready to stop wrestling with your thoughts and start rolling with them, grab this book, take a breath, and say it with me: *meh*."

—Helene Zupanc, licensed professional counselor & coauthor of *Sticky Note Mantras*

"As an author dedicated to exploring the nuances of mindful living, I'm often asked about practical strategies for navigating the daily onslaught of negative emotions. That's why I was so impressed by Hafeez Diwan's *The Power of MEH*. It's a brilliantly simple yet profoundly effective guide to reclaiming your mental space and finding peace amid the chaos.

"Diwan's concept of using *meh*—a shrug of indifference—as a tool for emotional disengagement is nothing short of genius. It's an accessible and relatable way to break free from the grip of unproductive thoughts and assumptions that fuel anxiety, envy, and self-doubt. The six-step process he outlines is clear, concise, and remarkably easy to implement in everyday life.

"What I particularly appreciate is Diwan's emphasis on self-awareness and his ability to integrate diverse ideas from psychology, philosophy, and even pop culture to support his arguments. This isn't about suppressing your emotions; it's about acknowledging them, understanding their roots, and then consciously choosing to *not* let them control you.

"While some might perceive the *meh* technique as an oversimplification, I see it as a powerful starting point for cultivating a more resilient and balanced mindset. It's a reminder that we have the power to choose our response to life's challenges, and sometimes, the most effective response is simply to shrug and move on. *The Power of MEH* offers a refreshing and practical approach to self-help that I wholeheartedly endorse. It's a book that will empower you to embrace a more contented and peaceful life, one *meh* at a time. If you're ready to take control of your emotional well-being, I highly recommend giving it a read."

—Adam J. Thompson, author of *Hard to Keep Happy: How to Maintain Lasting Joy in Challenging Times*

"We spend so much time trying to overcome external obstacles that we forget the biggest hurdles are often internal. *The Power of MEH* is a masterful guide for the rest of us, teaching a simple but profound strategy to outsmart the negative feelings that hold us back. A crucial read for finding the inner peace to persevere."

—Joe Sipher, author of the award-winning *Outsmart the Learning Curve*

"*The Power of Meh* uses a common word to attack complex problems—namely, how we let our thoughts consume us. As the author states, you can utilize the *meh* strategy 'to get past what blocks us . . . and . . . to loosen the grip of unhelpful feelings.' It's so simple that it just might work! Numerous applicable-to-real-life examples are given to show how to use the principle of saying *meh* to thoughts as a means of preventing us from having these thoughts have too much power in our brain space. While it might be apropos to say this book is meh—unfortunately, I cannot—it's anything but meh, and it's a tool I encourage everyone to try!"

—Jennifer Gold, MD, @gold_strategies13 (on Instagram)

"This word was not in my vocabulary, but it will be now. *Meh* is a verbal shrug, replacing negative thoughts with positive, affirming ones. And the book is a good read."

—Dr. John E. Wolf Jr., MD, MA, Professor and Emeritus Chair, Baylor College of Medicine, Department of Dermatology

"This book is an excellent reminder of what we should be prioritizing in our lives. Hafeez encourages us to use our ability to process our life experiences objectively (the meh effect) because it gives us control of our feelings. If we control our feelings, we have an opportunity to experience a higher quality of life. I can't stress enough the value of this message. I absolutely love the philosophy."

—Ray Stukes Jr., author of *The Self-Centered Perspective*

The Power of "MEH"
Feel Instantly Better, Contented, Fulfilled,
and at Peace—By Saying "MEH" to What's Bothering You

by Hafeez Diwan

© Copyright 2025 Hafeez Diwan

ISBN 979-8-88824-827-0

All rights reserved. No part of this publication may be reproduced, stored in a retrieval system, or transmitted in any form or by any means—electronic, mechanical, photocopy, recording, or any other—except for brief quotations in printed reviews, without the prior written permission of the author.

Designed by Suzanne Bradshaw

Published by

köehlerbooks™

3705 Shore Drive
Virginia Beach, VA 23455
800-435-4811
www.koehlerbooks.com

THE POWER OF "MEH"

Feel Instantly Better, Contented, Fulfilled, and at Peace—By Saying "MEH" to What's Bothering You

HAFEEZ DIWAN

VIRGINIA BEACH
CAPE CHARLES

DISCLAIMER: This book is not meant to be used and should not be used to diagnose or treat any medical condition. Neither the author nor the publisher is engaged in rendering medical, psychological, mental health, or other professional services or advice. If expert counseling is needed, the services of a competent professional should be sought. Neither the author nor the publisher shall be held responsible for any loss or damage (physical, psychological, emotional, financial, or commercial, including, but not limited to, special, incidental, consequential, or other damages) arising from any information or suggestions in this book.

TABLE OF CONTENTS

PART 1: GETTING TO KNOW MEH 1

PART 2: HOW TO MEH 11

PART 3: THE APPLICATIONS OF MEH TO
LIFE'S MANY TROUBLES 39

PART 4: MEH AND THE GOOD STUFF 111

PART 5: TWO FINAL POINTS 153

ACKNOWLEDGMENT 159

PART 1

GETTING TO KNOW MEH

THE MEH-NIFESTO

It is possible to feel instantly different—better, more relaxed, relieved, and at peace—by using a process in which we say *meh*, shrug off the feeling, and replace it with a more positive one. The process is easy and almost like "taking candy from a baby." The "baby," in this case, is the person with the feeling. The "candy" is the troubling feeling. Saying *meh* is equivalent to taking the "candy"—the feeling—from the "baby"—the person. Once the "candy" (the negative feeling) is removed, it can be easily replaced with a more positive feeling or idea.

The power of meh can be applied to a host of troubling feelings, ranging from anger to envy to boredom and dissatisfaction with our lives. It can help us deal with a lack of purpose and unproductive states of mind, such as pride, greed, stress, worry, and excessive self-interest.

The idea is to treat ourselves like we would treat a baby—that is to say, kindly, which includes taking away challenging, annoying "candies," those feelings, thoughts, ideas, and emotions that unnecessarily bother us.

In this book, we will explore how to apply the power of a simple *meh* in our lives.

Here is a summary of the meh process, or the "meh-nifesto":

When faced with life's annoyances, irritations, frustrations, and troubles, do the following:

1. *Watch* what you are feeling
2. Say *meh* to it
3. Ask yourself, "Why am I feeling or thinking what I am feeling or thinking?"
4. This will lead to the assumptions you are making about this situation and your reaction to it
5. Say *meh* to these assumptions as well
6. In the after-meh phase, move (or meh-ve) on to life with a more realistic and positive understanding of the situation

WHAT'S MEH (AND GOATS) GOT TO DO WITH IT?

We can start with a definition of meh: a response in which you shrug something off. Collins Dictionary defines it as reacting with "indifference or boredom." As an adjective, something meh could be dull, uninteresting, uninspiring, or not worth getting worked up about. Imagine a teenager confronted by an angry parent: "There are dirty clothes all over your bedroom! Is this the way to live responsibly?" The teenager answers, "meh," perhaps tilting her head, raising her eyebrows, and shrugging her shoulders.

The TV show *Melrose Place* figures into the history of the word meh (I have never watched *Melrose Place*—with apologies to fans of this show, I think of this show as *Meh-lrose Place*). Apparently, in 1992, a person commented on a *Melrose Place* online forum: "Meh... far too Ken-doll for me." You immediately sense that this person was not too impressed by the show.[1]

However, another TV show, *The Simpsons*, may be responsible for popularizing meh. In an episode from 1995, Marge Simpson tries to get her son Bart to weave, but Bart is not impressed. He says *meh* to her attempt to get him into weaving. In another episode from 2001, Homer Simpson wants his kids, Bart and Lisa, to go to a park, but they reject his overture with a meh.[2]

Another similar word that has popped up in the history of meh is "mnyeh."[3] Some think the word *mnyeh*, with a nasal emphasis on the M, is a form of meh. I think of it as a different flavor of meh. You can imagine saying to someone or something, "Mnyeh! I'm not impressed with you, whatever you are." But the message is the same with either meh or mnyeh, whichever form you prefer. Meh/mnyeh expresses the same kind of disdain and lack of being motivated or manipulated by some influence.

It is possible that the word originated from the Yiddish word "me," which sounds like meh.[4] Amusingly, this is where goats may play an interesting and possibly practical part in the history of meh. In his multilingual dictionary, Alexander Harkavy defines "me" as the sound of bleating or baaing.[5]

This is the goat connection, with the baaing and the bleating. Have you encountered a goat in the flesh? The one I remember vividly was a fierce, aggressive, and rude one. I totally sympathized with him because he was on his way to being sacrificed and eaten.

---

1 Nuwer, Rachel, 2013, " A 1928 Yiddish-English-Hebrew Dictionary May Be the First Official Record of "Meh" *Smithsonian Magazine*, September 9. https://www.smithsonianmag.com/smart-news/a-1928-yiddish-english-hebrew-dictionary-may-be-the-first-official-record-of-meh-5140610/
2 https://en.wikipedia.org/wiki/Meh#cite_note-Tribune-12
3 https://en.wikipedia.org/wiki/Mehcite_note-Tribune-12
4 Nuwer, Rachel, 2013, " A 1928 Yiddish-English-Hebrew Dictionary May Be the First Official Record of "Meh" *Smithsonian Magazine*, September 9. https://www.smithsonianmag.com/smart-news/a-1928-yiddish-english-hebrew-dictionary-may-be-the-first-official-record-of-meh-5140610/
5 Zimmer, Ben, 2013. "A History of *Meh*, from Leo Rosten to Auden to *The Simpsons* " *Slate*, September 6.

Surely, at the very least, a goat has a right to be rude to someone who wants to eat it up. I can imagine the goat saying, "You may eat me, you have that power, but I have the power to remain unimpressed by your power. I can be rude to you. I say, 'baa'! Bring it on, whatever you have! I say, 'baa'! Or meh!"

This illustrates some of the power of meh. Meh, as I mean it, is about shrugging off something that can pull you down, manipulate you, and make you less than what you can be.

What do I mean by this?

Read on!

GOOD MEH VS. BAD MEH—RULE NUMBER ONE: DON'T BE A PSYCHOPATH ABOUT IT

It is important to emphasize that I am not recommending that we turn into rude psychopaths.

There's good meh, and there's bad meh. Or I should say, there is *useful* meh and *useless, stupid* meh. Let me explain with an example.

Let's return to our messy teenager.

When the parent points out the dirty clothes in the teenager's bedroom, the teenager, who is rude or indifferent, says, "Meh!" Let's unpack this a bit.

You can use *meh* when you want to be a total jerk. It's possible. We can all avoid being useful or kind or helpful by saying *meh* to everything, no matter how serious it is. Children who need our attention, love, resources, and care—meh! Poverty, hunger, refugees, people in terrible situations worldwide—meh! Clearly, meh, in such cases, is an unkind, unfeeling, and unhelpful option.

However, even in the most horrible situations, a different kind of meh can be useful.

Come back to the messy teenager. The teenager could have low self-esteem issues and may consider herself worthless. She may be depressed. She may loathe herself. She may be pessimistic about life. She could be having a terrible day. Or she may be thoughtless, uncaring, or merely a teenager with too many other issues.

The parent confronts her angrily. The teenager could respond in one or more of the following ways:

1. Say *meh* and ignore the parent.
2. Feel like the whole world is against her.
3. Argue or fight.
4. Get mad and stomp out of the house.
5. Post on social media about how unjust or clueless her parent is.
6. And so on.

All these reactions, and others I haven't listed, are ways of letting off steam or coping with the parent's anger. But how about a *useful meh*? How would the teenager employ a *useful meh* in this situation?

Here's how I think of it (and how I wish I had known about it when I was a teenager!).

When the parent is angry, she says, "Meh."

But she does it to shrug off two things: the parent's anger and her immediate reactions.

Do you see what I mean?

The useful meh is a way to shrug everything off at the moment—the stimulus—good or bad—and your reaction to it—good or bad.

Contrast this with the *stupid meh*. Here, when we encounter a situation—a person, criticism, or things that go wrong or don't go our way—we say *meh* in frustration and stomp off (mentally and/or physically).

RULE NUMBER TWO: MEH IS A STRATEGY, NOT A WAY OF LIFE

My goal is to show you how to do useful meh-ing.

The most important thing is to realize it is a tool—a strategy, in the same way that using a toothpick is a strategy to remove an annoying particle stuck between our teeth.

Would any reasonable person keep jabbing toothpicks constantly or imagine that poking toothpicks is a way of life? Obviously not.

Similarly, useful meh is meant to be useful. We can't be in a useful-meh state twenty-four seven.

If we did, we might vegetate. If, whenever anything happened, we said *meh* and did nothing, and we did this 100 percent of the time, we might feel unbothered and unstressed, but then we'd have done nothing else.

But the idea of useful meh is to use it to get past something that blocks us. Meh is a strategy, not a way of life. It is to be used in certain situations. Situations that are hurdles. Situations that bog us down. Situations that can defeat us, crush us, make us powerless. Unless we use the power of meh.

This leads us to the next question: What are the situations in which we should use the power of (useful) meh?

WHAT'S A MEH LIKE YOU DOING IN A PLACE LIKE THIS?

Here's a simple rule of thumb for the situations useful meh can be helpful in: any non-life-threatening situation in which you feel pressured, anxious, disturbed, frustrated, or worried, situations in which you feel negative or even excessively positive.

Let's break this down.

Why non-life-threatening? Well, life-threatening or urgent situations that require immediate actions must be dealt with, of course. If a bear is charging at you or you are in a risky traffic situation, that's not a time for chilling out and meh-ing. You need to respond appropriately to survive.

Understanding why negative situations are perfect for useful meh is not difficult. Most people don't enjoy feeling awful, down, horrible, or like the whole world is against them. There's a story about a guy who bought a bag of red hot peppers, thinking they were sweet. He naturally realized how wrong he was when he put the first pepper in his mouth. They were uncomfortable and painful, but he continued to eat them. When asked by a concerned citizen why he was eating them, he answered that he wasn't eating the peppers. He was eating his money.[6]

Put yourself in this man's place. He has paid for the peppers. The peppers have value because of the money used to pay for them. Not eating them is like throwing the money away. That's throwing something valuable away (using his reasoning). And therefore, the logical conclusion is for him to eat every last pepper so he will get his money's worth (or so he thinks).

He can't stand to eat the peppers. They're unbearably awful to eat. He is losing sensation in his tongue and mouth. He is getting chest pain, not to mention gastritis. Life couldn't be worse. But he can't stop eating.

He feels pressured to do so because he doesn't want to waste his investment.

This is a situation that would benefit from meh.

He could simply say, "I've paid a lot for these peppers. So what? Meh!"

And that would be that. He could toss the peppers in the trash or give them to some soul who relishes them.

This man's situation is not very different from ours. We latch onto useless thoughts, worries, anxieties, and all kinds of

---

[6] Shah, Idries, 2015. *The Pleasantries of the Incredible Mulla Nasrudin*. ISF Publishing, Kindle.

mental baggage (or garbage) simply because we find ourselves unable to give it up. When you are feeling worried, the last thing you may be able to do is follow the advice of someone who tells you, "Don't be worried." How easy is that, in your experience? It rarely works because you can't avoid worry by forcing yourself to not worry. But you can use the power of meh, as I will show you in the pages to come.

But what about when you feel excessively upbeat, positive, full of energy, or simply amazing? Why meh in that situation?

My recommendation is to take advantage of the positive moments, use them, enjoy them, and relish them, but do so with the understanding that they won't last forever. Recall that pleasure and pain are two sides of the same coin, and often, highs are followed by lows. So please do enjoy the highs, but don't forget to meh. When you meh a high, you are saying, "I know what you are up to, brain [or mind]. Right now, I feel like a million bucks, but in a little while, without even realizing it, I might slip into a boring or possibly low feeling. That's okay. That's just the way you are, my dear mind. So, all I can say is that I am wise to your tricks. And here's what I say: Meh!"

This is very much like the story of a king in Idries Shah's *Way of the Sufi*.[7] The king wanted to "stabilize" his mental state. He asked his wise advisers to devise a ring to help him do so. His advisers came up with just such a ring. It was a ring with the words, "THIS, TOO, WILL PASS." Note that the king, for some reason, wanted therapy for *every* state, both the high ones and the low ones, precisely as I have recommended. We will come back to this later.

WHAT ABOUT GRIEF? A WARNING ABOUT THE USE OF MEH

---

[7] Shah, Idries, 2015. *The Way of the Sufi*. ISF Publishing, Kindle.

Meh is *not* suitable for grief, in my opinion.

When grieving over something, you may have to feel what you are feeling and work through it. I don't think it is a good idea to say *meh* to a feeling of overpowering grief. If you feel like crying or breaking down, so be it. Grief must be worked through appropriately, and I want to emphasize that this method is not applicable for it.

Even when you have other overpowering emotions, meh shouldn't be used to suppress these or push them under the rug. As we will see, watching our emotions and experiencing our feelings are essential parts of the meh process.

We shouldn't use meh to shut down our emotions or wall them off. That would be nuts.

Let's say you don't like an intense emotion that you are feeling. The natural tendency is to try not to feel it. And then comes someone like me who says, "Just say 'meh' to your emotion." This doesn't mean that we ignore it or attempt to block it. The temptation might be to say *meh* and move on. But don't do this. This is not what I am recommending, as I hope shall become clear to you very soon.

A useful analogy is with leaving the house. The proper way to leave is to go past the door and shut the door behind you.

Trying to wall off your emotions is like slamming the door in your face before you've left the house. That will leave you inside the house and would be a pointless move from the house-leaving point of view. This is similar to what happens when we try to *meh* past an intense emotion like grief.

When an emotion engulfs you, you need some distance from it, but the distance has to come gradually. You have to feel the emotion and then, slowly, slowly, try to watch yourself. How slow? Well, that would depend on the situation and the emotion. When my father passed away, it took me a few days to work through the intense grief, and then gradually, but surely,

I could safely take a look at it and watch myself grieving. But it may take much longer. For several months afterward, a sudden wave of grief would hit me. And I would let it hit me, watch it, and then move on.

As you will learn below, watching ourselves is the first step in the meh process, and it is essential and useful because it stops us from slamming the door and blocking out our emotions.

In the analogy of leaving the house, when you prematurely *meh* and try to shut the door in the face of your emotion, the house represents the emotion. You are in it. The way to get to the door is by wading through the emotion and watching it. That brings you to the "door." Opening the door means getting distance from the emotion. With that distance, you can say *meh*, as we will see later.

But how about the less intense irritations of life?

Some situations cause frustration, anger, annoyance, and so on: traffic situations in which we know there is no point in losing it, feelings of pessimism and disappointment that can bloom into full-blown gloom, and many other variations of feelings that can pull us down.

We know from experience that these feelings achieve nothing but make us feel bad for no reason. We can learn from experience when these feelings are about to rise and watch them come up. We can quickly move past them with the meh strategies you'll learn from this book.

PART 2

HOW TO MEH

AN OVERVIEW OF THE PROCESS

Meh is all about loosening the grip of unhelpful feelings and thoughts. To achieve this, some rather simple mental actions are required.

It all begins with a feeling, an emotion, a thought, an idea.

Step 1 is to take note of and watch whatever it is that is unhelpful or bothersome. If you don't even realize you have something that needs to be fixed, you're not going to do anything about it.

Step 2 is to say *meh* to whatever it is. This is a very simple thing to do, as you will see. The idea is to shake off the attachment to whatever it is.

Now you have some room, or space, between you and whatever it is that you are thinking or feeling. This allows us to go to step 3, which is to ask why. Why am I feeling or thinking what I am feeling or thinking?

In step 4, the answer or answers to this question come forth. Once you get the answers, you can explore the assumptions behind your answers. To use a nonsensical example, if the answer to "Why?" is "Because I don't want to be a broom," the assumption could be something as simple as "It's bad to be a broom." You get the idea. We will see plenty of examples of this throughout this book.

Step 5 is the second meh or the second cycle of mehs. We say *meh* to the assumption or assumptions. The idea is to push away from the assumptions and create some room for the next step. We regard all assumptions as false until proven otherwise.

Finally, in step 6, we are now able to think more clearly, calmly, realistically, and philosophically, in a way more in tune with the facts. We call this the after-meh. To continue using the silly example of not wanting to be a broom, our realistic thought might be, *Brooms are inanimate objects, and humans never become actual brooms*. In the after-meh, we grab onto any useful activity or thought process that can help us achieve the desired goal (which, in this case, would be to realize that humans are not actual brooms and vice versa). There is life after meh! And it is richer and more rewarding, as I hope you will see.

There is another step as well, like a fork in the road of meh. I will save it for last. I call it *blank meh*. It is a very powerful strategy, but it can seem like nothing (and in a very real sense, it is actually "nothing"). Not everyone may benefit from it (or appreciate it). I will go over it at the very end of the book. You can do just fine with steps 1 to 6. Blank meh is the icing on the cake, and if it appeals to you, you can certainly try it out.

In this book, we will spend the first part learning the basic strategy (steps 1 to 6). Then, we will study several applications of this skill to the many aspects of our lives—aspects that are, as I argue, not very helpful and often bad for us. Finally, I will end with "blank meh," which may not be to everyone's taste.

HOW TO MEH-DITATE

PART 1: HOW TO SAY MEH (AND FAKE IT, IF NEEDED)

How do we practice meh?

The practice is as simple as it gets.

Suppose you are in the grip of an unpleasant emotion or feeling: worry, anger, stress, boredom, purposelessness, dissatisfaction, etc.

In the face of such emotions, you have various ways of saying *meh*.

You can literally shrug and say *meh*. This may seem hard or idiotic. Or impossible. Ignore these feelings. Instead, simply shrug and say *meh*. As you say this, *pretend* that the awful feelings don't matter.

In reality, if you think about it, the awful feelings don't amount to much. They don't change anything. They certainly don't fix the problem or make it go away. A sucky situation gets suckier when you feel horrible about it.

And if you take the long view, feelings, even horrible ones, wax and wane. Of course, in the end, when we are dead and gone, our horrible feelings won't matter.

And so, if you *pretend* it's okay, not only is it okay, but it is also *effective*. You will be surprised how quickly you can get to feel some percentage of the meh you are pretending to feel.

Studies show that if you smile, you can make yourself feel

instantly better. The reason is that our brains react to our smiles by "thinking" that we are feeling good. And so, we feel good. It may sound ridiculous, but it is scientifically accurate.

Similarly, many people know that standing upright, confidently, or adopting the power pose can make us feel confident. You can hold your arms away from your body, stand with your feet apart, push out your chest, and move your chin upward—this power pose can make you feel more confident. When you are feeling a bit unsure of yourself, this move can perk you up and make you feel more in control of the situation. (Or so some researchers claim; others argue that it doesn't work, but it works for me, and there's no harm in trying it out, is there? See for yourself.)

My point is that a *pretend meh* can give you a tiny or heavy dose of meh. A feeling in which, when you say *meh*, what you are actually saying, no matter how negative, is something like this: "I remain unimpressed by you, negative or excessive emotion. To whatever you throw at me, I say, 'Meh. You do not sway me. You can do whatever the heck you want, but you are simply a bunch of chemicals running around inside a small group of nerve cells in my brain. And to you all, I say *meh!*'"

This may sound corny, but the mental effect of meh is one of remaining unimpressed, unmoved, and undeterred in the face of unpleasant mental energy.

You may be in a situation where you can't say *meh*. For example, you could be in a meeting, or you could be with other people who might get you committed to a psychiatric hospital if you suddenly burst out with a meh. What do you do then?

Well, all you do is an *inner meh*. A mental meh. A meh in which you imagine shrugging and saying *meh* with the appropriate feeling.

As I said, it's okay to pretend. Not only is it all right, but you may *have* to pretend. The reason is as follows: Our bad feelings are experts at making us feel bad. We are at the mercy of our feelings, we believe them, and we may dread them. But we have a secret weapon.

We don't have to believe them.

We can see through them. (They are impermanent, they have no staying power, they will go away—and we are only helping them on their way).

One way of putting a bad feeling in its place is to stare it square in the face and say, with fake confidence, "Meh."

Once you've said meh, even a pretend meh, to a feeling, you're on your way.

HOW TO MEH-DITATE

PART 2: TAKE A MEH-MENT— THE FIRST TWO STEPS

Saying "meh," physically or mentally, is all about taking control so that you or your mind can figure things out.

Essentially, you take a moment—or a *meh-ment*. And not just one but several.

Let us dissect the anatomy of meh and explore what is happening inside our brains. I don't possess a brain microscope and can't tell what's happening at a cellular, microscopic level. However, many experts who have studied psychology agree that it is useful to think of our minds as being composed of not just one mind but several.

We can call them "parts of mind," "baby minds," "mindsets," or even "mind-lets." It doesn't matter what we call them. The key point is that we don't stay in the same state forever, or even for that long.

States of mind, which can be either rapid emotions or lingering moods, come and go. I can safely state that I was upset sometime in 1974 when I was six, but the feeling has passed, and I don't even remember the particulars of anything that happened.

I am sure that almost everyone can relate to the fact that we pass through a series of mental states, none of which stick around perpetually. Even so-called constant moods may have fluctuations. For example, you may suddenly laugh because you find something amusing or bump your elbow and feel pain in the middle of a different mood. These mental blips can temporarily pull us away from the mood and into another state.

These mental states are like nannies. We could call them "nanny mental states." You may have heard the term "nanny state," referring to an all-encompassing or overprotective government that treats its citizens like babies and limits their choices and decisions. We could think of our mental states as *nanny mental states* because they encompass us completely. We are completely under the sway of our mental states. In this sense, because they control us totally, we could call our mental states "nanny mental states." They may have complete dominion over us, but we have ways of getting past the control of these mental nannies, which can, at times, be oppressive. One of the ways is what this whole book is about: the power of meh.

Consider the statement, "I am irritated." The *I* in this statement is essentially an expression of a nanny mental state. To emphasize this point, in this book, we will use *I* when referring to nanny mental states. For example, if *I* get annoyed by something, I have a nanny mental state that feels annoyed. When *I* feel happy, *I* have a happy nanny mental state, and when *I* feel peeved, *I* have a peeved nanny mental state. Each day, our *I* thinks and feels many different things. All these different thoughts and feelings are the products of different nanny mental states. We pass through many different mental nannies.

It may be helpful to think of these mental nannies as follows: In 1995 the psychotherapist Mark Epstein wrote a book titled *Thoughts Without a Thinker*. This title perfectly encapsulates the idea that we don't have a thinker separate from the thoughts being thought. Whatever thought we have depends on the mental state and is not separate from it. These mental states are like inseparable nannies of what we call our "self," or *I*. At any given time, a particular nanny mental state or *I* inhabits us completely. We are not separate from it. Whatever we think or do is from the point of view of the nanny mental state inside our heads at that point in time.

Here is an example of a random series of mental nannies that I went through. Each nanny mental state is the same as what *I* experienced in that moment.

NANNY 1/*I*	OMG! X happened! That's terrible.
NANNY 2/*I*	I'll have to do something drastic.
NANNY 3/*I* (sometime later)	Okay, it's not that bad. Bad things happen. Who said life was always about getting your way? Sometimes things go your way; sometimes they don't.
NANNY 4/*I* (sometime later)	You can't get caught up in hate. Isn't it better to love?
NANNY 5/*I* (sometime later):	Why don't I write a book about it?

Talk about living in a nanny state! The irony is that all of us, even those who hate nanny states, have a bunch of nanny mental states inside our heads.

The reason for making the distinction between what we call our "I" and our "nanny mental states" is simple. It is to remind us that there is no *I* that is separate from a nanny mental state. When our nanny mental state is positive, our *I* feels positive. When our nanny mental state is negative, our *I* feels negative.

Why should this matter?

Very simply, when we realize that our *I* is no more than a random, somewhat capricious nanny mental state, we have the option of not being swayed by it. We can swish these states by saying *meh* to them. Appreciating that our nanny mental states come and go, we can act on the positive, useful ones and discard the useless, unnecessarily bothersome ones using the meh strategy described in this book. Later, we will see many examples of this strategy in action.

Nanny mental states are different mental states that come and go without our willing them into being, and we believe them. Why shouldn't we? They are thoughts inside our heads, and we typically fall for the thoughts inside our heads. It seems natural, the way things should be. We unquestioningly accept and take up the mental attitudes that arise in our minds because that's how we are.

Consider the sequence of nannies I've listed above. I was lucky that I didn't stay wrapped up in the negative forever.

We all have some degree of ability to adapt, be resilient, and work with situations we dislike or loathe. But it can be a hit-and-miss business. Sometimes, we nurse old wounds and prolong our misery by thinking over and over about bad things that have happened to us. In such a case, our gloomy nannies keep feeding us miserable, unpleasant thoughts that turn our stomachs, ideas that make us feel yucky and awful.

Wouldn't it be nice to have a ring, like the king? A ring that says, "THIS, TOO, WILL PASS"? A ring that reminds us that all the gloomy mental states inside our heads can't keep us down forever?

Well, as it turns out, we do have such a ring.

Our magical "THIS, TOO, WILL PASS" ring can come in various forms (mindfulness, therapy, etc.). The form I am sharing with you has some features in common with the others. It is the power of meh. The first two steps of this process are as follows:

1. You watch yourself having a certain thought, listening to a particular nanny mental state.

2. After that, you say *meh*—physically or mentally.

Let us explore this in a little more detail.

Watching is essential. It's watching after the fact, of course, as shown below:

A nanny mental state comes upon me.

I feel the sting, but I decide to watch.

I watch the thoughts that are inside my head.

I watch and notice if I am feeling any sensations anywhere: in my head, my chest, my abdomen, or wherever.

I watch my thoughts and physical sensations closely.

When I watch, I enter another nanny mental state: the "watching" nanny mental state.

Immediately, as I watch, I get a teeny tiny distance from the nanny mental state that's bothering me (worry, anxiety, envy, hate, etc.). We will discuss this tiny mental distance in detail at many points in this book. For now, please note that *watching separates us from the nanny mental state, making us feel a bit better*. This separation is not like we've moved to another country. This separation is tiny, but it makes us feel a tiny bit better initially. But, as we practice it, we get better at it, and it feels a lot better.

The second step, the one in which I say *meh* to it, is when I declare to the annoying nanny mental state, "I don't believe you. I am not impressed by you. You're making a lot of noise right now, making me feel bad. But I know that you're here to come and go."

Observe what I have done.

I have taken control, a little bit. By watching myself react and flinging a meh in the face of the reaction, I have exerted a tiny bit of executive action.

It's like sucking the oxygen out of the flame of a noxious, irritating nanny mental state. The nanny mental state may linger for a bit, but it moves on if it doesn't get any support from me.

It gives me some time to figure stuff out and respond more reasonably.

HOW TO MEH-DITATE

PART 3: ASSUMPTIONS, MEH-SUMPTIONS— STEPS 3, 4, AND 5, MEH-ING OUR ASSUMPTIONS

We should practice saying *meh* to our assumptions as well. This is a critical part of the process.

Here is what I mean.

Suppose I am angry at someone for being thoughtless and stupid (or so I think).

Instead of getting angry, I could

1. Watch what I am experiencing in the mind and body, what I am thinking and sensing.

2. Say *meh* to what I find in myself—I have made a decision not to get pulled by the wave of an unproductive or negative feeling or thought.

3. Once I have a bit of freedom from the feeling, I simply ask myself, "Why is it making me angry?"

4. This will lead me to the assumptions I am making about this situation and my reaction to it.

5. Say *meh* to these assumptions as well.

One of my former colleagues is a wonderful person, known for speaking her mind and being very forthright. Her husband told an amusing story about her. When their daughter was little, her mother—my colleague—used to drop her at school. One day, her father took her to school. The daughter, very innocently, asked, "Dad, where are all the bastards?" Dad replied, "They only come out when your mother is driving."

We can break this story down to analyze what is happening at the assumption level. We will practice steps three, four, and five with the help of this story.

The mother drives the car; when drivers on the road drive badly, the mother gets upset and calls them "bastards."

Now, the question we ask, putting ourselves in the mother's shoes, is as follows: *Why? Why are they bastards?*

The answer is simple: *They are bastards because they are driving so thoughtlessly or stupidly or badly or selfishly.*

This can lead us to uncover the following assumption: *People who drive badly for whatever reason, be it carelessness, thoughtlessness, entitledness, etc., are bastards because the least one should do is respect other drivers and take the trouble to drive carefully and respectfully of others on the roads.*

Or you may think of some other assumption, but no matter the assumption, the way to meh the assumption is to say to yourself, *Even if it is true, is it worth getting my blood pressure up or losing any sleep over it?*

Even if the assumption is correct, it doesn't mean we should hurt ourselves by injecting hostility and negative emotions into our lives. There's a cost to being hostile. There is now a wealth of evidence that shows that hostility is bad for health.

As this anecdote shows quite plainly, not everyone has to have the same assumptions and react in the same way. The father, in this story, obviously thought differently about bad drivers. They didn't provoke him in quite the same way. His approach to them and his assumptions about them were different. Therefore, he responded differently.

Getting some perspective on our assumptions enables us to appreciate the importance of saying *meh* to them.

We say *meh* to assumptions, which is basically saying, "I don't care how correct you are, Assumption. You will not make me lose my cool and react to you in the usual way."

So here's what I say: assumption, meh-sumption! Some assumptions will be more serious and important than those involving bad drivers. And we may have to take steps to fix things. But we can do so without getting worked up.

Meh is all about getting the job done without getting worked up about it.

The importance of meh-ing assumptions cannot be overstated.

Assumptions are invisible supports for our opinions and feelings. If we question and evaluate our assumptions in light of more accurate facts, then we might drop our assumptions. Once we do so, our feelings and opinions would also be expected to change.

Don't take my word for it. Try the process out, and you will see what I mean. We will have many opportunities in this book to meh and eventually drop many assumptions.

PASSWORD ANALOGY

Have you ever changed your password—to your phone or some account?

If you're like me, you might keep entering the old password for some time because you are used to it. But then, gradually, you start using the new one.

Similarly, once you abandon incorrect assumptions, the old feelings and thoughts may pop up for some time. But when they do so, you realize that these are there from habit. And you quickly move them aside because there is no reason to keep them around.

Like old passwords, old feelings are no longer "used." Or believed. If you believed that you had to react in a particular way because of assumptions X and Y, once X and Y are proven wrong, then you have no reason to feel or think in the old way.

This is the reason why seeing through your assumptions is so helpful. This practice is essential for us to move beyond negative thoughts and feelings.

HOW TO MEH-DITATE

PART 4, CONTINUED: A SIMPLE, EVEN CHILDISH WAY OF MEH-ING ASSUMPTIONS

Being silly is a refreshing way to fight seriousness. Sometimes, we are grave, somber, serious, and disturbed by all the gravity and weight of the many burdens weighing us down.

For moments such as these, we can be silly, even for a moment, to lighten the mood and not get carried away by the wave of seriousness.

I will give you an example when it comes to assumptions. Almost any assumption may be countered with a silly, childish, *Na-na-na-na-na-na* meh.

Here is what I mean: Some people are obnoxious and can drive us to despair.

The assumption in this situation is as follows: I am frustrated because so-and-so is such a thoughtless, obnoxious jerk, and it is only natural to be frustrated when faced with such a person.

The silly, childish meh is to say, "So what? Scat! Shoo! I don't care if you are a correct assumption. You can be the most correct assumption ever, but I don't care. Do you expect I will make myself sick because of you, even if you are correct? Will the jerk miraculously transform into an un-jerk because I am giving myself an ulcer with all this reactive irritation?"

This silly meh is different from the stupid meh we discussed earlier. We are not shutting the door in the face of an intense, emotion-provoking situation here, trying to block our feelings. We are only facing the assumption, if it is a strong one, with a silly meh (as opposed to careful, well-reasoned arguments designed to defeat the assumption). It takes the wind out of the assumption's sails. This gives us the time to think more slowly and carefully about the assumption. As it turns out, this assumption is invalid, but we may need the time and mental space to think about it.

So, being silly is a step on the path to being wiser—or maybe only a tiny bit wiser.

HOW TO MEH-DITATE

PART 5: THREE HELPFUL IDEAS

I want to share three stories, thoughts, analogies, and ideas that may help.

IDEA NUMBER ONE

You may have heard the story of the scorpion and the frog. In this story, a scorpion approaches a frog who is about to cross a stream. "Help me get across. I can't swim. I'll climb on your back."

The frog is not so sure. "I can't do that! If I let you climb on my back, you'll sting me, and then we'll both drown."

"Don't you see how ridiculous that is?" the scorpion replies. "Why would I sting you? If I sting you, like you very correctly point out, we'll both drown. Why would I, a rational scorpion, do anything so stupid?"

The frog is impressed with the scorpion's logic. "Okay. Hop on."

While in the middle of the stream, with the scorpion on her back, the frog suddenly feels a piercing, painful sting. She feels her muscles weaken, and she begins to sink, and the scorpion begins to sink too.

"Why?" gasps the frog. "Why would you do such a thing? Why would you sting me? It makes no sense! Now we will both drown!"

"I know," the scorpion gasps as it drowns. "I know it makes

no sense! But it is my nature to sting, and I can't help acting out my nature."

Our mental nanny states are like scorpions. They can't help but be who they are. They are what they are. Our job is *not* to let the "scorpion hop onto our backs."

Here's how I would recommend using this helpful story.

When we notice an unhelpful, negative mental nanny state, we immediately watch it and don't let the scorpion-like mental state "hop on to our backs." The way to do this is to ignore it. Saying *meh* to it is one such way to *not* be manipulated by it. We may have to say *meh* several times, acting, pretending, and "faking it until we make it" (which works, as Dr. Marsha Linehan, among others, points out—we will meet Dr. Linehan later in this book).

IDEA NUMBER TWO

Following on the heels of the first idea, here's a superb thought that comes from Idries Shah in his *Darkest England*.[8] He uses the phrase "not letting the punch connect." He gives the example of a politician who avoids a tough question by answering another question he *wasn't* asked. The questioner's "punch" doesn't connect with the politician, who instead talks about a completely different, favorite talking point. Those of us who pay attention to the media may often come across several such politicians who are amazingly skilled at answering questions they have *not* been asked.

We can learn something from these politicians, but not about being liars or avoiding questions! No. Instead, we can learn the art of not letting punches connect. This is the same as not allowing the scorpion-esque mental nanny state to grab hold of us.

I want to point out that the "scorpion" will get close to us

---

8 Shah, Idries, 2020. *Darkest England*. ISF Publishing, Kindle.

and try to get a ride. This is unavoidable. We live in a difficult world, with vexing situations coming at us from all directions. We will react to a certain degree (a little or a lot). But with practice, we can notice the scorpion approaching. We will build the mental muscle that helps us watch and say *meh*. With practice, we will get better and better at it. And the punch will get less and less connect-y.

IDEA NUMBER THREE

In the same chapter of *Darkest England*, Shah quotes the following delightful verses from Sir William Gilbert (of the Gilbert and Sullivan team):

> On fire that glows
> With heat intense
> I turn the hose
> Of common sense
> And out it goes
> At small expense!

I fell in love with these verses the first time I came across them in the late eighties. They are, I think, simply marvelous.

Here's how to turn the hose of common sense on the fire that glows with "heat intense." First, you've got to notice that there is a fire. That's the watching phase. That's when you spot the negative nanny mental state, like the fire (or the scorpion) suddenly popping up on the scene.

That's when you put some distance between yourself and the fire/scorpion. You do this by saying *meh*. You remain unimpressed and unmoved by the coming onslaught. You don't let the punch connect. You don't let the scorpion leap onto your back.

HOW TO MEH-DITATE

PART 6: AFTER-MEH

Okay, now we have gone through the first five steps of the process.

In step one, we watched what was happening to us.

In step two, we said *meh* to what was happening inside us.

In step three, we asked why this was giving rise to our feelings.

In step four, we found the assumptions causing us to feel the way we feel.

In step five, we said *meh* to the assumptions.

Now we have had two rounds of meh: first, to get some distance from a feeling, thought, emotion, etc.—a nanny mental state—and second, to get some distance from assumptions that sit at the root of that particular nanny mental state.

This has brought us into a mental clearing, a space of some kind, where we can obtain a different perspective that hopefully helps us respond with less negativity. When I say respond, I mean respond both mentally and physically.

The mental response is *different* from a disturbed, negative, irritating feeling.

The physical response is more intelligent and calm, in a balanced, undisturbed, and un-rocked-by-some-negative-state way.

In after-meh, we reflect more usefully on ourselves and the situation in which we find ourselves. Freed from the tyranny of the feeling or opinion that is tying us down, we accept something—anything—useful. And use it to help us. It can be a helpful thought, strategy, activity, etc.

HAPPY MEH-RRIAGE

When we pass through a nanny mental state, we assume that the state is "me." In a way, this is true. The nanny mental state is inside us, inside our heads. So who else would it be but me? There is no one else inside our heads. But if we think a bit more, we may come to the realization that it is unnecessary or not totally correct to think that the nanny mental state is *all* of me or what I am, *completely*. There are several reasons for this.

First, we routinely pass through many nanny mental states in a day. Many of these are very different from each other. We can ask, *Are they all me?* It seems more accurate to say that they are all *parts* of me. Many psychologists observe that we act as if we have multiple minds inside us or, to put it in another way, multiple *I*s. As discussed previously, we cycle through multiple nanny mental states or *I*s all the time.

Second, we all have stomachs and noses. But we don't automatically think that if we have a stomachache, that stomachache is the same as me. Likewise, when we have colds, we don't equate our colds with ourselves. We don't say, "I am my stomachache" or "I am my cold."

We feel much more personal about our thoughts, however ridiculous they are. And so we assume that no matter what nonsense we are thinking, it's important and true. Of course, we can all appreciate it when we have been stupid or doubtful about some of our thoughts. But in general, we tend to believe them, including our opinions about people, movies, politics, etc.

When I have a stomachache, I say, "I have a stomachache."

Understandably, I will try to do things to get rid of my stomachache.

When I have a thought, I might say, "I have a thought."

But I won't necessarily try to get rid of this thought unless it is something absurd (e.g., a thought that there might be a giant panda hiding inside my lunch box). Most thoughts appear reasonable, logical, or maybe even excellent. When I cast my vote for the candidate of my choice, I think I am making the best choice. When I conclude something, I think I am correct.

We are biased. The result is that we accept emotions of like, dislike, anger, irritation, frustration, enthusiasm, love, completely pro-something, or absolutely anti-something else.

If you have any doubts about this, look at the number of swings of opinion we have in our lives: for people, stocks, movies, books, businesses, etc. We fall in and out of love with all sorts of things. If our thoughts were always stable and constant, people would live happily ever after, and there would be no divorces. Here's an example.

STEP 1: Two people fall in love; their nanny mental states converge on a feeling of "love" or "This is Mr. or Ms. Right."

STEP 2: The intensity of feelings of love decrease; their nanny mental states now register "Nothing new here" or "Blah" (or "Meh!").

STEP 3: Other things happen. More information comes to light. Annoying habits that were overlooked in the past become more noticeable. The parties fall out of love. One or the other has an affair, etc. Their mental states now declare, "This is most definitely *not* the person or marriage I like. In fact, I hate my life."

The changing attitude/mental state is the result of two

things: changing circumstances (more information or an affair) and a changing mental state, irrespective of the circumstances or information.

Think of it this way. We don't usually stop loving our kids because they've been horrible. Our love for them usually remains (there are exceptions). This is not the case when spouses grow apart and end up hating each other. The reason for this is biological; biologically, what we feel for our kids is not what we will ever feel for another person.

And this is my point, exactly. For biological, physiological, and neurochemical reasons, our nanny mental states are fickle. They change, jump around, and take us with them. This is why we fall in and out of love.

It is as if every nanny mental state lays a claim on us, and very often, we unthinkingly go along with it.

So, a nanny mental state shows itself as "*I* am feeling/thinking this/that." Most of the time, we immediately accept that this is the way things are. We believe our thoughts. We accept them without question. This can be a problem if the nanny mental state is an unhelpful one.

Here's where meh comes into all this. I recommend that meh be used to break the hold of the mental state, especially when the state is causing too much distress, angst, anger, pessimism, gloom, or negativity.

We get married to our views, opinions, feelings, emotions, and moods until we fall out of love with them. And then, we fall into other views, opinions, feelings, emotions, and moods.

Instead, if we married our mehs, our "meh-rriages" would be happy. Meh gives us the ability to stop a nanny mental state. Next time you feel like so-and-so is a total jerk for cutting in front of you, bring the power of meh. Say *meh* to your anger, to the thought filling you with hostility. Use meh to get some space between you and your emotions and nanny mental states.

WHAT'S AN EMOTION ANYWAY?

Lisa Feldman Barrett's *How Emotions Are Made* is a useful read.

Dr. Barrett makes a compelling argument that emotions are learned. This surprised me because we all hear about universal emotions and how they appear on the face. It is assumed that we are hardwired to detect and express universal emotions (anger, fear, disgust, and surprise).

However, Dr. Barrett argues that different emotions may appear the same. We often mistake one emotion for another (such as confusing fear and anxiety). In an interview with *The Verge* (April 10, 2017), she noted that when it comes to telling what emotion someone is feeling, whether negative or positive, "people mistake all the time without the context. When you take a super positive face and stick it in a negative situation, people experience the face as more negative."[9]

In other words, we use context clues in order to read emotions. If you see a photo of someone with a "positive" expression in a "negative situation," the facial expression is seen as "more negative."

There was also an interesting point made during this interview about the "resting bitch face." People understand this to mean an expression viewed as irritated, annoyed, contemptuous, and unfriendly. Dr. Barrett has studied the resting bitch face phenomenon. Her conclusion? It is a "neutral face." She explains, ". . . structurally, there's nothing negative in the face." So why do we see a neutral face as a bitchy expression? Dr. Barrett answers that people use "the context or their knowledge about that person to see more negativity in the face." In other words, if you have a poor opinion of someone, or if the situation seems negative, you might view a neutral expression

---

[9] Chen, Angela, 2017. "Neuroscientist Lisa Feldman Barrett explains how emotions are made." *The Verge*, August 10. https://www.theverge.com/2017/4/10/15245690/how-emotions-are-made-neuroscience-lisa-feldman-barrett

as a "resting bitch face."

We interpret an observed emotion in the context of the situation and what we think of someone. But how is an emotion made? How do we construct our own emotions? This is where I find Dr. Barrett's ideas incredibly insightful.

The simplest way to understand her point of view is to use the old expression "monkey see, monkey do." In this instance, as we grow older, we see and learn "emotion concepts." After seeing and learning, we express and "do" the emotions.

Babies feel certain things. They learn from their parents that a certain feeling is "anger" or "sadness" or that they are "hangry" or feeling "fear." They feel certain things in their bodies and minds, then add the emotion concept to what they have learned. As they grow older, they pick up many emotion concepts from the adults in their lives.

I saw this with my children. There was a time when my daughter started expressing "anger" in situations in which she had previously not expressed anger. Initially, there was a time lag between the situation and her response. For example, the situation happened, and then a brief moment (a second or two) passed. Then, she made an angry face and used an angry tone. I noticed the same with "sadness" or when she was "upset." A moment after the situation, the expression of "sadness" or "upset" arrived.

In other words, she had learned from others (parents, friends) that this situation called for a particular emotion. She had learned emotion concepts and applied them in the appropriate setting.

This is incredibly liberating. It means that we react in certain ways to certain situations (traffic, losing, being thwarted, etc.) because we have learned to apply certain emotion concepts to those situations. The liberating part is that we can learn to respond in other ways.

Two examples may make this point clearer.

THE MAN WHO HAD HIS CAR STOLEN

Many years ago, my father and I encountered a man whose car had been stolen. He wasn't unhappy or upset about it. On the contrary, he appeared happy. He was smiling. Both my father and I were puzzled. Our "emotion concept" applicable to this situation was that when your car is stolen, you should be upset. It's only natural, right?

Well, not for this guy. I asked him, "Why aren't you upset?"

His response? "What's there to be upset about? Things get stolen."

I still find this rather strange. But strange or not, it is a more useful response. Imagine being liberated from the shackles of "having to feel bad or upset." Being upset is not going to bring his car back. It's only going to make him feel miserable. So what's the point of it? Why not learn something different? Why not learn to feel okay when a car (or something else) is stolen? If only we could learn this magical trick, it would be pretty amazing and liberating, wouldn't it? As it turns out, we may be able to do this with meh (more on this later).

THE STRANGE CUSTOMS OF AN ODD LAND

The second example is something I learned from someone as a child. I don't remember the person who told me this. It might have been my nanny (ironically).

There was a mythical place where people were overjoyed when someone died and cried when a baby was born. Why? Simply because life is such a pain! Someone born has to go through the same sorry situations and deal with pain, suffering, and disasters. And these troubles more than cancel out any joys experienced in life. Thus, it made sense to weep for the little one about to be thrust into life's chaos and distress.

In contrast, for the one who is dead and gone—what a lucky

person! She no longer has to deal with the angst, irritation, or horrors of life. The people were ecstatic that their dead companion had escaped from life's mess.

I don't know if such a place truly exists, but you can see how their "emotion concepts" led them to express emotions that are the opposites of what we consider normal. Imagine how less disturbing life would be if we could learn to modify our responses to awful situations. I am not recommending we turn into cold-blooded psychopaths who revel in the deaths of our companions and loved ones. I am merely pointing out that from a theoretical point of view, the idea that we construct our emotion concepts and then act on them sets us on a path to a bit of freedom from them. It gives us the potential to escape from mildly irritating or truly debilitating emotions.

PART 3

THE APPLICATIONS OF MEH TO LIFE'S MANY TROUBLES

In this part, we will explore the uses of meh in our lives, particularly as it relates to our mental trouble: upsets, perturbations of our mental equilibrium, disturbances of the mind, mental chaos. These troubles can be physically and psychologically unhealthy, which is why operating without them can make us happier and more creative.

Ready? Let's go.

TROUBLE 1: PRIDE

Pope Gregory regarded this as the worst of the seven deadly sins. The title of one of Jane Austen's books suggests that pride is linked to prejudice.

Most of us have a favorable view of ourselves. In common with others, I like myself, think I am better than others in many ways, and I believe that I understand things better than others. Even if I feel that others make excellent points, I may still find my points more appealing.

This may be a design feature common to most humans.

Our love of ourselves and our opinions, feelings, and ideas seems inbuilt.

It has been argued that if we knew how insignificant we truly are, we might get depressed and fall into a state of dark despair. Given a slight change in circumstances, the environment, or body chemistry, we can cease to be useful or even alive. Many lives have been cut short in the most tragic of ways, and no matter how wonderful we are, we are at the mercy of being extinguished by accidents, illnesses, or calamities at a moment's notice. Approximately 150,000 people die each day, and while two-thirds of these are age-related, none of us are getting any younger as the days pass by, and so one of these days, we will be the ones dying.

But we don't think of ourselves as being at death's door. Most of us (excluding those who are clinically depressed and those who have a low opinion of themselves for whatever reason) think very highly of ourselves. I had a professor who used to joke about another colleague, saying, "Professor So-and-So is a legend in his own mind." The truth is, we are all legends in our own minds.

So, what's the problem with excessive pride? (I want to emphasize that this refers to pride as in arrogance or being too full of oneself. There is a healthy kind of pride, which is more like satisfaction or a feeling of self-respect, of being "enough" and worthy of respect without having to justify oneself to others. In this book, we will be considering troublesome pride and arrogance, not the healthy one.)

1. It often—actually invariably—comes before a fall. It's true. We are genuinely not as amazing as we think we are, and when we realize this, the realization can be shocking. If you think you are a hero, then discovering that, in reality, you are closer to zero can be devastating.

2. There's no good reason to be proud. Pride is a stance at odds with the truth. I remember this delightful story of meatballs who discover, with horror, that they are about to be eaten up. I can imagine myself as a proud meatball, in awe of myself and how superb a meatball I am. And then, I find out that I am about to be torn apart by sharp teeth inside a mouth full of bacteria, saliva, dental plaque, and food stuck between teeth. No matter our accomplishments, we may feel a bit proud, but the proud *I* will taste a final defeat. This is as true for the wealthiest, most powerful humans as it is for the poorest and weakest among us.

3. Pride (that is to say, arrogance) doesn't make sense. Some people say feeling proud is okay when you do a good job. What's wrong with that? Why not feel proud when your kid does well? Or when you accomplish something truly extraordinary? There are two problems with this way of thinking.

    a. First, what if none of these wonderful things happen? What if you never do anything out of the ordinary? What if you are, at most, a solid average? What if you are below average? What if you are a worthless shmuck? Should you feel the opposite of pride? And what if, after achieving great things, you lose your level of expertise and become barely adequate? Now, with nothing to feel pride about, will you think that you are not worthy? Any ideology or way of thinking that accepts pride makes a huge mistake. It gives you a measurement, a score, based on your performance. It says that you must be worth something to be worthy of pride. This kind of pride is often called "authentic," but I don't understand what this means. To me, it seems like an authentic mistake. It is a mistake in which a misleading and erroneous feeling is believed to be correct.

b. Why is it misleading? Here is the second problem: All of us, without exception, are here not because of anything we did. We were born one day and found ourselves on this planet. We each have a particular genetic makeup. Some of us grew up in well-to-do circumstances, and others in awful ones. Depending on the mix of our genetics, our environment, the people around us, and luck, some of us will do amazingly well, some will do well, some will do okay, some will do not so well, some will fail, and many will be total flops in life. Very few things are under our control, and even those under our control (like discipline, working hard, perseverance, grit, etc.) depend on our minds and bodies being able to function—and that is most definitely not under our control. So, we are, at all times, working on borrowed hardware. Nothing—*absolutely nothing*—in this world is truly our own, not even that thing called *I*. So how can there be any pride? In a sense, we don't exist, apart from the combination of factors that give rise to us and allow us to continue existing. Since we are not here, in a manner of speaking, who is the chap or chappess who feels pride? I admit this is an extreme way of thinking. But our ability to achieve depends entirely on things we can't control, so there can be no "authentic pride" in something we achieve—since even what we achieve is utterly dependent on our being alive and healthy.

4. Jane Austen was right. Pride *does* lead to prejudice. In her book, two people who have a chance to have a great life together nearly don't come together. Why? Here's a summary (and I apologize for the spoiler alerts): The hero is proud, full of himself. In his imagination, he surely deserves someone better than the plain, unremarkable-appearing heroine. Why? Because he is so great, he deserves someone outstanding. This prejudices—biases—him against the heroine. For her part, the heroine is also proud. He is not good enough for her. He is too vain and, therefore, less than what she is willing to accept. Her pride also prejudices her. This connection between pride and prejudice is real. If we are proud and prejudiced against an inferior-sounding, unappetizing truth, we may (or will) pay the price for choosing a "superior" fake over an "inferior" truth.

History is littered with examples of people who were too proud to make a wise choice. Dictators were too proud to accept reality (such as Hitler, Mussolini, Saddam Hussein). Political pundits may have been too proud to think that Hillary Clinton could lose to Donald Trump. Prime Minister David Cameron may have been too proud to think that Britons would vote for Britain to leave the European Union. The Nobel Prize-winning physicist Ernest Rutherford may have been too proud to think that one could make power from an atom (he called the idea "moonshine"). The folks who thought the *Titanic* was unsinkable and didn't take common-sense measures could have saved many lives. Many of the unfortunate passengers on the *Titanic* may have felt quite proud of making the historic journey on the ship.

Or any number of us, with our personal histories, can surely think of times when we made the wrong choice because we were too proud.

For example, have you ever felt too proud to apologize? It has often been said that in a marriage, you can either be right or you can be happy. Trying to prove you're right about some issue (even if you are) can endanger the prospects of a happy union. If you think about it, it is smarter to be happily married, with all its health, psychological, and sociological benefits, than it is to prove how right you are all the time.

Pride is a classic example of an overarching nanny mental state, convinced it is superior and better than others. The result? *I* think *I* am great, better than others, inimitable, excellent. Even those who don't have much in a material sense can be proud. They can be proud of the fact that they are so much better than the vain, superficial folks who may have a lot but have many flaws, don't understand anything, and will eventually have to give in to disease and death, and how will their money save them then, huh?

Functionally, there is no need to think about pride in an overly dramatic way. It is merely a nanny mental state in which an *I* thinks it is better and right-*er* than others. Every *I* thinks in this way. It has to. After all, the job of the *I* is to look after itself, to look out for its interests. A proud *I* is thus a logical way for the *I* to be, from its point of view.

So, what can be done about pride? As you may have guessed, the strategy is *meh*.

When you find yourself feeling oh so full of yourself, here are the steps to combat this:

STEP 1: Take note of the feeling. How does it feel inside your head and body? What sensations do you have? How do excessive self-importance, an exaggerated sense of worth, and self-righteousness feel?

STEP 2: Pride is a nanny mental state, bubbling in several nerve cells inside your brain. It is the stuff that dreams are made of, and how wimpy and wispy are dreams? They can be blown off easily. So, repeat after me. "Meh. I know you are just a momentary aberration inside my head. You are like a wave in my mind, a self-important one, but you don't have staying power."

STEP 3: Ask yourself, "Why do you think you are better than others?"

STEP 4: The assumption is this: Because the thought inside my head is telling me so, the thought must be true.

STEP 5: Say *meh* to the assumption. You think, *Really? How can I be sure that every thought inside my head is true?* Therefore, you say *meh* to the assumption—unless it's proven to be true. Assumptions are not inherently correct; they must be proven.

STEP 6: After-meh: Play with the assumptions and think more accurately about them. You can now allow correct, realistic thoughts into play. Are you that great? Truthfully, the evidence is against it, as shown above. Thinking you are great can cause you to make stupid decisions. It can make you avoid the truth and miss opportunities.

My recommendation, which I try to follow, is to ask myself, "Is the way I think about something based on pride? Do I feel too big to accept a small-appearing, supposedly inferior truth?" Here's a real-life example. I must be an absolute fool, but I thought that Amazon and Netflix couldn't be successful. Looking back, I could have purchased stock in these companies and made a profit, but I didn't. Why? I was too proud. How?

I thought the founders of these companies and the analysts favoring them were mistaken. They were missing what I assumed was the obvious truth, that Amazon and Netflix could not be successful. It didn't make sense to me, because I was (and remain) quite ignorant of how businesses and the economy work. I lacked the foresight to appreciate the power of these and other businesses. I could see things only through the lens of my prevailing mindset, which was fairly limited in this area.

I was too proud to imagine that I could be wrong, in the grip of a nanny mental state that imagined it knew more than it did. So, I missed out on a great investing opportunity. Such is life!

But, as the poet Saadi reminds us, we should learn from the mistakes of others so others don't have to learn from ours.

So don't be like me. Every so often, do a pride check. Are you missing out on an important truth because you are too proud?

TROUBLE 2: SELF-ESTEEM

There are two opposing points of view: First, that self-esteem is necessary and good. And second, that self-esteem is bad.

On the one hand, if you have a low opinion of yourself, that is hardly a good way to be. Feeling worthless can depress you and make you pessimistic. Pessimism can make you physically sick. Heart disease, high blood pressure, and anxiety are associated with pessimism. A low opinion of yourself—low self-esteem—can, therefore, be harmful to you.

On the other hand, if you are full of yourself, have gobs of self-esteem, and think you are amazing, then you may suffer from pride. And pride, as we have seen, is a problem.

We can easily appreciate where the two sides are coming from. Those who are pro-self-esteem see the effects of low self-esteem and naturally conclude that self-esteem is necessary and needs to be built up. And those who are anti-self-esteem naturally conclude that it is not a good thing to be a proud, arrogant ass, and therefore, self-esteem is not good for you.

Which of these points of view is correct? Both of them.

People who esteem themselves too much have pride. They need to consider the problems of pride and apply the corrective strategy.

For those who suffer from a lack of self-esteem, the power of meh may be helpful.

STEP 1: Watch the feeling of not being good enough or unworthiness—low self-esteem—when it arises. How does it feel inside the head and the body? What sensations does it produce?

STEP 2: You say *meh* to the feeling (either loudly or mentally, depending on whether you are alone or in company).

STEP 3: Next, you ask, "Why am I feeling low self-esteem?"

STEP 4: You answer, "Because I am nothing compared to others and feel I am unworthy. If only I had quality X or accomplishment Y, I would truly be something."

STEP 5: Say *meh*. Assumptions are not inherently correct; they must be proven.

STEP 6: After-meh: Play with the assumptions and think more accurately about them.

In reality, this is a nanny mental state convincing the *I* in this scenario to achieve X or Y before the *I* feels worthy. Do you think that's true?

If I do poorly on a test, I may feel low and incorrectly conclude I'm unworthy. I may get the same message from my family and friends, who expect me to "be" better (which boils down to "do" better). Or I may have internalized what I imagine society expects of me. Or I may have formed the impression that I am not a valuable member of society. All these result in low self-esteem.

The problem is not that *I* am worthless but that I believe the thought that I am.

There are plenty of unaccomplished individuals in the world. Are they worth nothing? Suppose you come upon a homeless person talking to himself, occasionally shouting, and punching an invisible enemy. Will you say to yourself, "Look at this useless fellow! What has he accomplished in this world? He is a pointless, worthless waste of a human being"?

I am positive that most normal human beings will not say anything like this. They may not even feel anything like this. They will probably feel sorry for this poor fellow.

The same could be said for any number of disadvantaged or incapable people who don't accomplish the kind of success we look up to.

In other words, someone who has achieved nothing is not worthless. If we connect this to ourselves, we conclude that even if we have achieved nothing, we are not worthless or failures.

Most people with low self-esteem think and act as if they don't believe this. But is there a good reason not to believe this? I don't think so. Therefore, when one is in the grip of low self-esteem, one could say *meh* and then move past the limiting assumption.

There isn't a connection between worth and accomplishments. Every life is worth something simply because it is a life.

Therefore, the solution is to immediately *meh* our mistaken thoughts and assumptions.

The way I picture it is to tell someone who has low self-esteem, "You think you are not worth anything. The truth is, you are valuable because all humans are equally valuable. You just *have a thought* that you are worthless. It's like *having the thought* that there's a monster beneath your bed or a dinosaur out in the yard waiting to eat you. Here's how to deal with this thought."

Then, explain how successive waves of thoughts rule our minds and that we should not fall for them. Or use the shorthand phrase: Don't believe every thought you have.

TROUBLE 3: CONTEMPT/LOOKING DOWN ON OTHERS/JUDGING OTHERS

We often look upon others, and others may look down upon us.

We may adore someone who we think is great, but we can sometimes judge people we consider "others" (those who are different from us, who think differently than we do) or those we criticize for falling short of greatness.

Sometimes, the looking down can reach the level of contempt. This can happen in marriages, for example. Dr. John Gottman has studied this and shown that contempt for a spouse can be a sign that the marriage might fail.

I suppose we have to evaluate the people and conditions around us. This makes us successful at assessing situations and responding to them appropriately. However, we can carry this useful skill into areas where it is not needed—or helpful. After all, there doesn't seem to be a survival or adaptation advantage to judging the poor singing of an artist.

You may say, "I can see that contempt is not a great thing to have. But what's the problem with being a little judgy when a player plays badly or a singer sings poorly? It's only a bit of harmless fun."

We know we are being judged, and we go to great lengths to avoid criticism. We should always try our best, but doing so only to avoid judgment is not a pleasant feeling. It is possible to do well without being motivated by the fear that "it will look bad if we don't perform flawlessly." And when we judge others, we are aware that we, too, will be judged, buying into the dynamic of constant societal judging.

I wish we could stop judgment altogether. No such luck, I'm afraid. But I am saying that if we drop the judgmental mindset, we won't care.

When we stop judging others, judgments become less important to us. They don't matter to us that much. And so when somebody scorns our skill, we will shrug it off. Meh.

If you don't judge, it won't matter to you if someone judges you.

The famous saying "Judge not, that ye be not judged" means that if you don't judge others, God will look kindly upon you and not judge you harshly. However, it could also mean that judging will become less important to you when you don't judge.

An analogy might help. Imagine that, as a society, we were obsessed with how many beads we had. We would look down upon someone who had only a few beads. But this would make us vulnerable to the criticisms of others when our bead supply dwindled. However, if we didn't care how many beads someone had, it would imply that beads mean nothing to us. If someone were to say to us, "You only have two beads," it would mean absolutely nothing to us. We would say *meh* and move on.

So, we need to become nonjudgmental.

STEP 1: Watch the feeling of being judgmental, scornful, contemptuous, etc., when it arises. How does it feel inside the head and the body? What sensations does it produce?

STEP 2: You say *meh* to the feeling (either loudly or mentally, depending on whether you are alone or in company).

STEP 3: Next, ask, "Why am I feeling judgmental or contemptuous?"

STEP 4: You answer, "Because the person is not doing a good enough job. They deserve to be looked down upon. Some people are excellent and deserve praise, while others deserve criticism."

STEP 5: Say *meh* to these assumptions (unless you can prove them). Assumptions are not inherently correct; they must be proven.

STEP 6: After-meh: Play with the assumptions and think more accurately about them.

Simply because someone "is not up to the mark" doesn't mean we should judge them. What makes a person is a mixture of their nature and nurture, their genes and upbringing. I can only do what I can, given my makeup; this is the same for others too. For example, no matter how hard I try, I can't suddenly increase two feet in height, sprout another finger, or become a flawless football player. With some effort, I may achieve a marginal ability in football, but I am not very big and over fifty, so there's a limit to what I can achieve.

Suppose that I were to try my hand at football and play adequately (spoiler alert: there's no chance of that happening!), and suppose further that some team was to be insane enough to hire me. I am sure I would be exposing myself to criticism and judgment. The team would be judged too. The fans would be livid. They would most certainly fume. Who hires someone like that? That player is awful, and so on. Yes, judging is inevitable, but the situation is inevitable too. Given the raw material—us—certain outcomes are unavoidable. Judging is futile because people can only achieve what they can achieve, no more. If they could have achieved more or something different, they would have.

When you think like this, you will be unlikely to judge simply because you will understand that it makes zero sense.

If you are responsible for changing or improving someone, like your children or students, how about doing so nonjudgmentally? I can't imagine judgment changes anything. It is extra baggage. You can present the option or the right circumstances if you want change or improvement. You can explain, "I think you may be able to achieve this. How about giving it a try?" You can encourage, motivate, and give pep talks, but you should do it realistically. That is to say, it is up to the child or student to do the best she can. Judgment creates resentment, whereas a lack of judgment promotes appreciation.

Being judgmental doesn't add; it subtracts. And it makes you susceptible to the judgment of others.

TROUBLE 4: PERFECTIONISM

While writing this book, I was conscious of its need for editing before publication.

Typically, I obsess over mistakes. No matter how hard I try, some mistakes—including some pretty big ones—remain undetected.

Why do I worry about these mistakes? Simple. Perfectionism. I want the book to be perfect—that is to say, perfectly free of errors. I don't want people to see it and say, "What a sloppy writer!" or "What bad grammar he has," or pick fights with the ideas. And therefore, I read and reread the book *ad infinitum*—which made for a pretty miserable time, I can tell you that.

Most of us would agree that a book shouldn't be full of errors—it can be pretty distracting or downright annoying when a book is poorly edited and full of mistakes. But after reasonable efforts have been made, it is time to let go.

Perhaps you can think of examples from your life, and if you can't, congratulations!

Perfectionism has gone too far. It can cause anxiety because you want to get the work done—but can't because you want it to be perfect. If you are part of a team, your perfectionism can drive the other team members mad—unless they are perfectionists as well, in which case the job may take forever to complete, or it may remain uncompleted.

Perfectionism is a nanny mental state in which the *I* strives to achieve a perfect product. Since perfection is unlikely to be attainable, this *I* remains chronically dissatisfied. And the job remains unfinished. Or if it is finished, the *I* feels embarrassed or ashamed or stressed out about what people will say about the work. Or because the *I* thinks *I* should be perfect, *I* feels inadequate or unworthy.

So, when perfectionism gets you down, here is what you can do.

STEP 1: Watch the feeling of trying to be perfect when it arises. How does it feel inside the head and the body? I usually feel a burning sensation in my stomach and sometimes a tension headache. You may not be able to pin down what you feel or be able to articulate it. It doesn't matter. Simply watch and take note of whatever you think and feel.

STEP 2: Simply say *meh* to the feeling (either loudly or mentally, depending on whether you are alone or in company).

STEP 3: Next, ask, "Why do I want to be perfect?"

STEP 4: You answer, "Because we should all try to strive for perfection. I will feel bad if I make mistakes, and society expects me to be perfect. I don't want to fail or look bad."

STEP 5: Say *meh* to these assumptions. Remember, you have to prove them. Assumptions are not inherently correct; they must be proven.

STEP 6: After-meh: Play with the assumptions and think more accurately about them.

First and foremost, nobody's perfect. We are what we are. And we are *not* perfect.

Also, ask yourself, "What is perfect?"

Perfection may mean different things to different people. If you are doing a job, someone might think it is okay to make a mistake in the process if the result is a completed product. But another person might want a perfect process. Some authors might arbitrarily decide it is okay to have one typo every 150 pages, but another might say there should be zero typographical errors.

Do you like to eat insects? Probably not. Do you like chocolate? If you do, you should realize that an average bar of chocolate contains eight insect parts. The Food and Drug Administration says that eating anything less than 60 insect parts per 100 grams (about two bars) of chocolate is okay. This is because it is impossible to eliminate cockroaches (or their poop) from cocoa beans; the only way to do so is to use tons of pesticides that are more dangerous than the insect parts.

Trying to get rid of insect parts from what we eat is impossible. According to Dr. Morton Teich, an allergist at Mount Sinai School of Medicine, the only way to do so might be to stop eating altogether.[10]

Imperfection is everywhere. No matter how hard we try, we can't be perfect, especially since the criteria for perfection are so loose.

Consider love. One person might assume perfect love is

---

10 The Body Odd (Life's Little Mysteries staff), 2012. "Chocolate allergies linked to cockroach parts." *NBC News*, April 2. https://www.nbcnews.com/healthmain/chocolate-allergies-linked-cockroach-parts-628784).

receiving all twelve of the gifts in "The Twelve Days of Christmas," whereas another may strive for affection instead of gifts.

And what you believe today may differ from what you thought ten years ago. Maybe you had a crush during adolescence. Do you still have that crush? When you were sixteen, you may have thought that life without that crush would be imperfect, incomplete, and disastrous. Do you still feel the same way? Probably not.

It is hard to determine, from the inside, whether something is correct. Stepping outside the current state to objectively observe, meh, put the wrong ideas in their place, and approach a more reasonable idea in the after-meh is often what's needed. In the after-meh, we see that

1. Perfection is subjective.
2. Perfection is probably impossible, since even our most perfect food items may contain insect parts, and how lovely is that! Given the number of insect parts in food items, eating a full, delicious meal might be the equivalent of eating a fraction of a small roach.

Given this understanding, the push for perfectionism can be seen as attempting to be something you're not. None of us will lose sleep trying to transform ourselves into a cat. We will not succeed in teaching sheep to recite Shakespeare. Likewise, we will never be perfect, especially since we don't even know what perfect is.

Since we can't always trust our gauge of what is considered perfect, since perfectionism is inherently unachievable, and despite society—or even you—wanting you to be perfect, we must push ourselves to try to do our best, finish the job, and move on.

To quote an often-used Voltaire phrase, "Don't let perfect be the enemy of the good." The most we can do is a good enough job. And let that suffice.

TROUBLE 5: LACK OF SELF-COMPASSION

When I write, I set a simple goal. For me, the goal is to write for twenty to thirty minutes a day. The idea is to do the minimum amount I set for myself, and if I go over, there is nothing wrong with that.

But, being human, I sometimes struggle to reach the minimum time or even to get started. When I fail, I feel bad. I criticize myself for not reaching my goal.

And when I have a day off, or it's the weekend, I grow irritated with myself that I didn't get it done. I had all this time off, yet I accomplished nothing.

These are small examples of not being compassionate to oneself. I am sure you can think of many others. We can all be hard on ourselves when we fail to reach our goals.

Regret over a missed opportunity can cause self-blame and anger, sometimes for years.

Lack of self-compassion is linked to many negative, unpleasant results. People can feel shame or guilt because they failed. Or they can become anxious, sad, or depressed.

A lack of self-compassion is a genuine problem, but it is fixable with a small adjustment.

Ironically, while writing this, I found this section tough. I had just had lunch, followed by an enormous chocolate chip cookie, and no doubt, the influx of food slowed me down. Too much food puts me in the mood for sleep or makes me lose my edge. The self-guilt only proved to me that this section could impart something to me, just as I hope it does to those who read it.

STEP 1: Watch the feeling of trying to be perfect when it arises.

How does it feel inside the head and the body? I feel like I am frowning on the inside or annoyed. You may not be able to pin down what you feel or be able to articulate it. It doesn't matter. Just watch and take note of whatever you think and feel.

STEP 2: Simply say *meh* to the feeling (either loudly or mentally, depending on whether you are alone or in company).

STEP 3: Next, ask, "Why am I uncompassionate with myself?"

STEP 4: You answer, "Because I haven't accomplished what I set out to. I should be able to do more, be better. This needs to get done, and I am to blame."

STEP 5: Say *meh* to these assumptions. Assumptions are not inherently correct; they must be proven.

STEP 6: After-meh: Play with the assumptions and think more accurately about them.

It is possible to draw a straight line from pride, through perfectionism and self-esteem, to lack of self-compassion. Pride says, "I am terrific," which leads to "I should do this perfectly." But we may fall flat on our faces. Failing is a blow to our self-esteem. The root of self-esteem, low or high, is the "self." If there were no self, would there be any self-esteem or need for it?

So, with failure comes a nasty jolt to self-esteem. The result is negative self-talk—"You failed, you stupid, useless thing! You needed to do more and better, but you didn't"—which leads directly to a lack of self-compassion.

The corrective strategy is to understand that when we are hard on ourselves, we only fill ourselves with negative emotions. Nobody wants to hang out with a crabby, negative person. When that crabby, negative person is inside your head, it becomes difficult to run away from yourself, maybe even impossible. You are there, wherever you are, and if you are in the grip of toxic nanny mental states, there's not much you can do about it. Or so it seems.

But it is untrue.

You can say to yourself, "These thoughts are doing nothing but causing me pain. So meh! Off you go, scat, shoo!" A little secret about nanny mental states is that they have no sticking power. They are just neurochemical bursts inside our brains, and we can use the power of meh to disable them. If they rise again, we simply say *meh* again as many times as it takes.

We can only do what we can do. We are what we are. If I could have been a king or a billionaire, I would've been one, but I am stuck with being who I am. And, when I get right down to it, that's not such a bad thing. I can breathe, walk, bathe, brush my teeth, eat, and do a million other things that all lucky, healthy human beings can do.

So there are two valuable strategies: First, we have to be grateful for who we are, and second, we can dispute the assumptions.

There is no "should be able to do more or better" or "must do this or that." Remember the story of the meatballs? No matter how great we become, we are like the meatballs: destined to be eaten. We, too, are destined to be the food of worms (or bacteria). We have some time to do a few things, and all we can do is what we can do. Yes, we need to get things done, but the only control we have is on the efforts we make. (And even those efforts depend on us being alive and healthy enough to make those efforts.)

Have you ever felt so sleepy that you literally couldn't do anything? Or have you ever fallen sick and been unable to move? Is there anything you could have done at that time? Would you have been able to "do more or better"? Did you ever say to yourself then, "Even though I can't get up, I am going to do this task?" It is more likely that you wouldn't have cared for anything in the world but to sleep, rest, and recover.

And so, once we realize that it is only an overbearing thought that makes the *I* feel bad that such-and-such task remains unfinished and therefore *I* am to blame—well, we can simply say *meh* to it and all the assumptions that this *I* depends on. And when we do so, we can see the actual situation: We can only do so much. And if we fail, that's because, statistically speaking, we will fail at times (and succeed at others). That's just the way things are.

TROUBLE 6: PROCRASTINATION

What I wrote in the previous section could be used as an excuse. You could go to the beach and say, "Well, I am what I am, and this is what I am. I want to enjoy myself. One day, I will be dead and gone. What's the point of getting worked up about anything?"

But if you have children, a family, or people who depend on you, you can't go to the beach for the rest of your life. (I mean, of course, you can do whatever you want to. But I assume you have responsibilities and need to do things to ensure your life doesn't sink into chaos.)

If you are like most people and aren't abandoning life's demands, procrastination is probably a part of your life. The word comes from the Latin *procrastinat*, which means *deferred until tomorrow*. But as we all know, tasks are often deferred much longer than tomorrow. (Chronic procrastinators would be thrilled if they could defer only until tomorrow!)

Procrastination has several problems:

A. The work doesn't get done on time (or at all in worst-case scenarios).

B. The procrastinator feels anxiety, pressure, stress,

irritation, and frustration from having the work "hanging over their head."

C. The procrastinator may feel guilt and shame, blame herself, and display a lack of self-compassion.

D. The procrastinator may feel that he can never get anything done, that he is useless, and then fall victim to low self-esteem.

E. Others may judge and be critical—or downright mean—to the procrastinator.

What about procrastination itself? Can we do something about procrastination?

Many excellent books show how to deal with procrastination. There is an interesting equation about procrastination. It's called, unsurprisingly, the procrastination equation and is very helpful. It comes from Dr. Piers Steel, who has written a book on the topic (more about it soon). For the moment, let us tackle procrastination in the usual way:

STEP 1: Watch the feeling of procrastination when it arises. How does it feel inside the head and the body? To me, it feels like a yearning, a mental itch that makes me want to do something else—anything other than what I am trying to procrastinate. You may not be able to pin down what you feel or be able to articulate it. It doesn't matter. Simply watch and take note of whatever you think and feel.

STEP 2: Simply say *meh* to the feeling (either loudly or mentally, depending on whether you are alone or in company).

STEP 3: Next, ask, "Why do I want to procrastinate?"

STEP 4: You answer, "Because I really don't feel like doing this task right now. It doesn't need to be done right away, so what's the rush? I'd rather be doing something else, so I'll be distracted and bored."

STEP 5: Say *meh* to these assumptions. Assumptions are not inherently correct; they must be proven.

STEP 6: After-meh: Play with the assumptions and think more accurately about them.

What is a more realistic approach to procrastination? There may be more to not doing a task than merely wanting to do something more fun. Many experts have recognized that fear of failing or falling short may be at the root of not tackling tasks.

If I can't do it perfectly, then I don't want to do it.

And so we have perfectionism intruding here. We can use our anti-perfectionist meh strategy to remind ourselves, "Nobody's perfect or even agrees on what perfect is," and then we can move on to the notion that we shouldn't let "the perfect be the enemy of the good."

The truth is, no matter how fabulous we are, someone can always find fault with us. So why not get the job done if we can?

Dr. Steel's procrastination equation is *Motivation = Expectancy x Value/Impulsiveness x Delay.*

The *expectancy* is where perfectionism comes in. If you expect to do well in the task and are confident that you can do it well, you will be more motivated. This makes sense. However, if you think you aren't up to the task or will do the job badly, you will be less inclined to do it. A delayed term paper or project might have something to do with the fact that you don't feel you can do a good job. In this case, remind yourself to meh your need for perfectionism. Don't merely say, "Don't let the perfect be the enemy of the good." Instead, say, "Don't let the good be the enemy of the adequate," or even, "Don't let the adequate be the enemy of the not very good or probably bad." In other words, don't judge how bad it will turn out. Meh perfectionism, meh being very good, meh being adequate.

The second part of this equation is *value*. I assume that the task has some value and importance. If it is important, you have an additional reason to say *meh* to perfectionism and the desire to do a fantastic job. Yes, you may not be solving an earthshaking mathematical problem, but just go ahead and do your taxes already as correctly as you can! The task has value. Not doing it will cause you pain in the end.

We can now argue with the other assumptions behind procrastinating.

Assumption 1: *This task doesn't need to be done right away.* Really? The *delay* in the procrastination equation refers to how far out the deadline is and how long it will take to see the results of your actions. If the deadline is a year away, there is less motivation to do something. If flossing today means healthier teeth in the long run, you may keep putting it off, saying, "If I don't floss today, it's okay. I can always floss tomorrow. It's not like I will get gum disease tomorrow if I don't floss today."

The flossing example is helpful because it illustrates a point that we often ignore or forget. We cannot predict how much time we will have to do something tomorrow, three months, or a year from now. Chances are that we will probably have as much time as we have now. Or less. Or more. So, if we have time now, *now* may be the time to do something that has value, even if the deadline is way out and the payoff (no gum disease) is also way out.

And it's not like you have to finish the task right away. You can simply commit to spending a few minutes with it each day. A few minutes is all it takes to get you rolling. Once you get past the hurdle of "I have to do it perfectly," you can do a little bit each day.

Assumption 2: *What's the rush? I'll do it later.* This is a variation of the above, and you can apply the same arguments. Remember, "later" will probably look very similar to "now," and the task will appear as unattractive "later" as it does "now." The only difference will be this: You may feel more stressed later because the deadline will have moved closer. So why not do it now?

Assumption 3: *I feel like doing something else, so I'll be distracted and bored if I do it now*. Read between the lines here. What is this assumption really saying? It says I won't be able to do the task well. That's perfectionism, so meh perfectionism. That's the first thing to do.

The other aspect of this is impulsiveness, wanting your rewards right away—immediate gratification. Suppose you have a source of fun, and you still have time before the work is due. If you are impulsive, you may grab the fun, hang out with your buddies, surf the web, or seek immediate gratification rather than the task that will provide delayed gratification.

So, how do you deal with the fun-loving part of you? What do you say to it? I would recommend tricking it. That's the easiest way. I do this all the time. Here's how.

I say to myself that I will do this annoying task for a short time, and then I promise I will do all the fun stuff. This method is called "good procrastination." I learned it from Roy Baumeister's book *Willpower*. It is a very effective and easy method. Once you trick fun-loving you, you will be propelled by the momentum of your actions. For me, it was writing this book. Even though I am enjoying it, I had to use good procrastination to get it done. Because writing it wasn't as enjoyable as binge-watching a good show. And do you know why a part of me doesn't want to write? Because I keep feeling like I am not doing a good enough job. And I keep saying *meh* to this feeling and the assumptions behind it. Meh. Meh. *Meh*.

So when you'd rather be doing something fun (who wouldn't?), practice this. Say, "Yes, what you are doing may not be that great. But who cares? Do it anyway. It can't be that bad. And even if it is, you can only do what you can. You are what you are."

Assumption 4: *This is a very boring task.* Okay, I get it. Some things are genuinely boring. When it comes to boring stuff, I trick myself with the "good procrastination" strategy. I say, "Yes, it's boring, but do it for a few more minutes and do the fun stuff after."

And there is a way to make boring stuff interesting (more about this later, in the section on boredom).

TROUBLE 7: STRESS

Stress is a state of overwhelm. There is too much to do and too little time. Or we may lack the resources—mental, physical, and financial—to tackle the situation. Or there's too much information, and we find ourselves unable to absorb, retain, deal with, or work with it.

I like a saying from Idries Shah, which I have found to be very useful in dealing with feelings of overwhelm and stress. The quote is as follows: "Even a hen has a short and flat ruff to sit on, so that it doesn't get in the way. But your mind can be so full of long and short, hard and soft thoughts, that they stick out all over the place, interfering with thinking itself."[11]

I like this saying because it captures the essence of stress. Too many thoughts run around in circles inside our heads, stressing us out. The thoughts could be variations on the following: I have to do laundry, but I also need to do dishes, take out the trash, get the mail, and return those clothes that don't fit. Oh, and those have to be returned today. But I also need to cook dinner!

Too many thoughts, all jostling inside our stuffed skulls, make it difficult to have a moment of peace or rest.

We all know that stress is harmful to the body. Here is a partial list of problems associated with stress: anger, anxiety,

---

11   Shah, Idries, 2020. *Observations*. ISF Publishing. Kindle.

chest pain, depression, doing drugs, drinking, inability to focus, lack of motivation, headache, irritability, muscular pain, not eating enough, overeating, sadness, sleep problems, smoking, stomachache, and withdrawing from others.

Here is a partial list of diseases associated with stress: acid reflux disease, asthma, colds, diabetes, heart disease, high blood pressure, irritable bowel syndrome, and strokes.

Needless to say, stress is not good. However, experts say that a little bit of stress may keep us motivated. I suppose it is "good" because of the value and delay parts of the procrastination equation.

We are more motivated to do something when we value it. So, if something is important and there's a time crunch, we may be more motivated to accomplish it.

While a little bit of stress can motivate us to complete something, it is healthier to learn to manage stress. So, how do we manage it?

Many excellent books and articles have been written about this topic. This book's focus is on thwarting negative feelings, opinions, and assumptions. So, let's do this.

STEP 1: Watch the feeling of stress when it arises. How does it feel inside the head and the body? I feel multiple things: a burning sensation inside the pit of my stomach, a tension headache, and muscular aches and pains. Simply watch and take note of thoughts and feelings.

STEP 2: Simply say *meh* to the feeling (either loudly or mentally, depending on whether you are alone or in company).

STEP 3: Next, ask, "Why do I feel stress?"

STEP 4: You answer, "Because I need to do all these things and don't have the time or capacity to do them. If I don't succeed, there will be chaos. There's nobody to help me, and it drives me crazy."

STEP 5: Say *meh* to these assumptions. Assumptions are not inherently correct; they must be proven.

STEP 6: After-meh: Play with the assumptions and think more accurately about them.

There are two chief ideas in this book: You are what you are. And you can only do what you can do.

This means that no matter how hard you try, there's only so much you can do.

Reflecting back to Shah's saying, how do we get a flat ruff like a hen? It's not complicated, and we've been doing it all along. We have been saying *meh*. This or that thought can pounce on us and consume our brain space, but we can shrug it off and say *meh*.

The idea is to disregard these long, short, hard, and soft thoughts. When we meh, we pay no attention to them, essentially shooing them. They may not go away, but we can glance at them, ignore them, and move on to something else. This way, we start clearing our mental space for the after-meh phase. Hopefully, we get ourselves a short, flat ruff and can think a little better.

Faced with an army of thoughts or demands, we observe our nanny mental states, shoving all these tasks in our faces. They depend on the assumptions given above. Let's question them:

Assumption 1: *All these things need to be done right away.* Yes, but remember, we are what we are. Human beings. Until we change into problem-free multitaskers, we can only do one thing at a time. Multitasking is unhelpful. It can make us miss important details. If the situation is important, it can seriously damage how well we handle it, leading to mistakes. Since part of our brain space is taken over by another task, multitasking diminishes focus on one task.

Most of us can comprehend that certain things are

impossible. We can't go to that lovely pastry shop in Bruges, Belgium, while getting our shoes repaired in Mobile, Alabama. We can understand that and don't spend too much time or mental energy trying to figure out impossible tasks. Why? Because it is a stupid thought, and we know it's pointless. When we understand how useless certain things are, we stop hankering after them.

A little help for focusing on a task comes from the late Umberto Eco, who wrote many books, including the extraordinary *Name of the Rose*. In this book, the hero and his assistant have only a few hours to solve the mystery, or they'll face a catastrophic outcome. The hero tells his assistant that they have to work as if they have all the time in the world. This is a form of cheating, mental cheating, in which you lie to yourself. But what's the harm? Things may be going to hell, but if you need a sharp mind to work with, you can't dull or inflame it with tension and stress. Even if you have no time, pretending you have all the time in the world to focus on a tough task is better than having a nervous breakdown, becoming agitated, and being unable to think clearly because you are so stressed.

Assumption 2: *If I don't do all of these tasks, there will be chaos.* Of course, this assumption may be valid, but there's an unspoken assumption behind this one. It is hiding in plain sight. The assumption begins with *If I don't do all these things*.

The assumption is that I **must or can** do all these things. That may be true, but if you have to be simultaneously physically present in Alabama and Belgium, that is impossible. You know that, so you don't bother to say anything like this.

It takes practice to try to focus on one task at a time without distractions. It's like threading a needle. It takes concentration, and if we are worried about feeding the cat or taking the car to be repaired, it will take us much longer to thread the needle.

The solution is to be real. When we accept that certain things lead to poor outcomes, we automatically stop doing them.

Assumption 3: *There must be somebody or something to help me.* It would be nice, naturally, to have help, but sometimes that's not possible. Life is unfair (we'll learn more about meh-ing this later), but we must be realistic. This assumption is incorrect because there is no rule that says we must have everything we want (in fact, life shows us that, quite often, we don't). As Dr. Albert Ellis, the founder of rational emotive behavioral therapy (REBT), said, "There are three musts that hold us back: I must do well. You must treat me well. And the world must be the way I want it." The key point is that any assumption that has the word "must" in it should be questioned because there is a reasonable chance that it may be wrong.

When we are short on money or resources, we can spend time crying over what we don't have, but eventually, we have to move on and work with what we *do* have. I think it's perfectly okay to have a mini bitch-fest within yourself: *Why is life like this? Why is there crisis after crisis? I just want to scream! AH!*

Go ahead and get it out of your system. And then, after you have decompressed, say, "Okay, now how about I focus on the task at hand as if I have all the time in the world?"

You do this because you realize this is the best way to get results. You are trying to thread the needle of your problems, your tasks, and the many things you must do.

Your problems will not magically disappear, and you may not find a fantastic solution immediately, but if you put your mind to it and think calmly and with focus, you may just crack it.

The solution to stress is to ignore the multiple issues, say *meh* to them, shoo them away, focus on the most important thing first, and work our way down the list with focus and clarity.

We can add the element of gratitude when we work our way down the list. We should reflect that being able to do things, even little things, is pretty amazing. We have to be in good enough health and have the resources and ability to do things. Not everyone is lucky enough to perform tasks. When we inject gratitude, it gives us a good feeling, a little boost to our mood and spirits, making the to-do list a little easier to go through. To rephrase Mary Poppins, a spoonful of gratitude makes the stress go down.

OTHER HELPFUL STUFF

Since stress is such a huge problem, there is a wealth of information about this. We can meditate, exercise, practice mindfulness, take time off regularly, and be with family and friends. They are tools that can help us recharge and stay healthy.

But what do you do when you have very little time? We focus on what we are doing, no matter what it is. We give it our undivided attention. When we focus on what we are doing, we practice mindfulness.

This is essentially a form of meditation. When we think about how we will solve a problem, we are meditating on the problem. We often think of meditating on a mantra or a word, but meditation is a moment of focus on anything, even our problems. We can say to ourselves that we are going to focus on our problem and use it as an object of our meditation. When we do this, we are mentally cheating ourselves into thinking we have time to focus on one thing. It provides a short break. It can be like taking a walk for a few minutes, offering momentary relief.

Finally, relationships are a big part of mental rejuvenation. While we can't be with friends and family all the time, we are often around people, whether at work or in the community. A simple smile to a stranger can provide a pleasant interaction and help boost the mood of everyone involved. Or smile at yourself in the mirror instead. It still works.

TROUBLE 8: GREED

Imagine I am concerned about insufficient money to meet my needs. My *I* in this situation sees things through the filter, the lens, of this nanny mental state. *I* is convinced that the solution is to get more money—more, more, more, to meet my needs. This results in greed.

Or, another example. Got too much pride? Most of us do, to some extent. Once we understand how it works, we can easily see that pride is mixed in with many other problems, including greed. And believing you are superior to others means you believe you deserve more in life (greed).

We latch on to several "best" things in life: money, sex, food, luxurious houses, first-class travel, season tickets, etc. The list is different for different people.

Once you approach anything with greed, you are feeding the nanny mental state, making the *I* want more, more, more, no matter what:

A. *I* is not happy or content because it is in a state of grasping and discontent.

B. It puts the person into situations and actions designed to get what *I* wants.

C. Failing to get what *I* wants can cause distress—a lot or a little.

Is this a pleasant way to be? Wouldn't it be better if we weren't greedily going after this or that, working ourselves into a frenzy?

On the flip side, *I* may get what it wants—hooray! Or is it hooray? We know that getting what *I* wants doesn't solve anything. *I* quickly gets bored with what it got and wants something else now. Robert Burton wrote the following in his 1621 book *Anatomy of Melancholy*: "A true saying it is, *Desire hath no rest*, is infinite in itself, endless, and as one calls it, a perpetual rack, or horse-mill." This describes the hedonic treadmill, where *I* keeps going after something, then something else, and then something else perpetually.

I have noticed this behavior in myself. I love a good book, but more than a good book, I love the idea of buying one. I've had this desire since I was a kid, when I used to beg my mother and sisters for money to buy more and more books. This process hasn't ended. Forty years later, I still crave beautiful books to buy. The dopamine burst lasts for a few days; then I want another.

It's good to read books and learn from them. But it is annoying to have to keep buying books to feed the hunger.

So, greed is a state that causes distress and discontent, and it doesn't end. It's an addiction. So, what is the poor, greed-afflicted one to do? Very simple.

Next time you feel the greedy impulse arise (I am speaking to myself too), do the following:

STEP 1: Watch the impulse. How does it feel inside the head and the body? What sensations does it produce? I feel a "want" in the left side of my chest; it's hard to describe. Simply watch and take note of whatever you think and feel.

STEP 2: Simply say *meh* to the feeling (either loudly or mentally, depending on whether you are alone or in company).

STEP 3: Next, ask, "Why am I feeling greedy?"

STEP 4: You answer, "Because I really want this. It will give me happiness."

STEP 5: Say *meh* to the assumptions. Assumptions are not inherently correct; they must be proven.

STEP 6: After-meh: Play with the assumptions and think more accurately about them.

Is it true? Does getting wealth, or whatever we want, give us happiness?

Once the feeling of greed becomes less intense, while it is whimpering away with its tail between its legs, remind yourself of the futility of greed and how it can almost never be satisfied.

Some argue that greed is good because it makes you go after things you need. Really?

Here is a partial list of problems caused by greed, listed by Arthur Nikelly:[12] anxiety, depression, insomnia, moodiness, fatigue, social isolation, temporary joy, and despair.

Whatever the greedy person wants or gets brings only temporary relief. It does not last. No wonder the poor soul feels despair. But since it is an addiction, the cycle keeps going on: The greedy one goes after X, gets X, feels temporary relief, feels horrible again, goes after Y, gets Y, feels temporary relief, feels horrible again.

Does this seem like a pleasant recurrence?

As the poet Saadi wrote, "Poor greedy one, wherever he runs. He's after food, and death is after him."[13]

So, instead of greedily grasping after this and that, how about realizing the whole sorry business of greed? And go after this or that in a more balanced, reasonable, not greedy way. Go after it with a plan without getting worked up or anxious.

We won't stop needing things, but do we have to have an annoying addiction to go after them?

TROUBLE 9: LUST/DESIRE FOR PLEASURE

Lust feels good. However, the pursuit of lust and pleasure suffers from the same problems as greed.

Lust is responsible for us being here. The lustful impulses of our ancestors in distant times led to reproduction, which led to us. Our desires have led to our children, and the cycle continues.

---

12   Nikelly, Arthur. 2006. "The Pathogenesis of Greed." *International Journal of Applied Psychoanalytic Studies* 3 (1): 65-78.
13   Shah, Idries, 2021. *The Dermis Probe*. ISF Publishing. Kindle.

But uncontrolled lust is not good for society.

Lust is part of the hedonic treadmill. We chase an object, get it, get bored, chase another, and so on. We can't keep our dissatisfaction away for long. Lust is a type of greed, greed for pleasure, the type that gives a feeling of bodily or mental pleasure, relief, or ecstasy.

But it is a short-lived sensation.

Sex addiction can take a severe toll on a person. It can cause the person to compulsively chase after sex, perhaps at the cost of other responsibilities, present dangerous risks and sexually transmitted diseases, and lead to shame, guilt, anxiety, depression, and substance abuse.

It can disrupt marriages and relationships and lead to social isolation.

The excessive pursuit of any form of greed can be harmful to society. Some people may prosper, and many others may suffer. Lust, unchecked, is responsible for the following problems in society: prostitution and the objectification of vulnerable women, men, and children, sexually transmitted diseases, child pornography, adult pornography, sexual slavery, and dangerous sexual pursuits that can harm others.

Lust hijacks a sexual need (or some other pleasurable need) and blows it out of proportion. Healthy gratification of such needs, within boundaries and limits, is perfectly okay. But when the matter goes out of bounds, even if it feels good and gives temporary relief, it can be very dangerous.

How do we apply meh to lust?

STEP 1: Watch the feeling of excessive lust or desire for pleasure when it arises. How does it feel inside the head and the body? You may feel a grasping sensation, a yearning, a feeling like you deeply desire something. Simply watch and take note of whatever you think and feel.

STEP 2: Simply say *meh* to the feeling (either loudly or mentally, depending on whether you are alone or in company).

STEP 3: Next, ask, "Why do I feel excessive lust?"

STEP 4: You answer, "Because I desperately want to have sex or gratification. People should satisfy their desires. If I suppress mine, it can harm me."

STEP 5: You say *meh* to these assumptions. Assumptions are not inherently correct; they must be proven.

STEP 6: After-meh: Play with the assumptions and think accurately about them.

Most of us understand that it is not okay to satisfy every desire we have. One person's desire and lust can end up hurting everyone involved.

Excessive suppression of desires can undoubtedly cause problems. Trying to cut ourselves off from *all* desires is unhealthy. Repressing or suppressing desires is harmful. But this doesn't mean we should give in to every desire.

So what can one do? If you can't suppress or express your desires, what can you do?

What if someone has excessive desires, lust, or wants? What then? What is the solution?

If you are a sex addict or are lustful to a pathological degree, then it makes sense to seek professional help. But if you don't have a problem needing such help and only want to have a "good" time, then you have to do the following:

Understand that the pursuit of a "good" time can easily lead to a bad time.

Understand it is an addiction.

Realize that you can't suppress or block your desires.

Keep repeating this process. It takes practice. Nanny mental states are all bark and no bite. When you don't give them attention, they wither away.

TROUBLE 10: ENVY

Unlike pride and greed, most people agree that envy is a real pain.

The envious person is greedy; they want what someone else has. They may feel inadequate or inferior, lacking self-esteem. "If I had a billion dollars, I wouldn't feel like such an unaccomplished bum—and all my former classmates and colleagues would get sick with envy."

The envious one wants to provoke envy in others. They want others to feel the same psychological and physical pain as they do. Envy feels uncomfortable in the mind and body. I experience it as a burning feeling in the left side of my chest.

Once envy makes its home inside our heads, it may inspire us to get what we think will make envy disappear and make us equal or better than those we are trying to measure up to, provoking envy in other less successful ones. Feeling envious can indeed increase our drive to do better. Studies show that envious people may be a bit better at their jobs than those who are less envious, but this doesn't mean that we should be envious so we can be better workers.

Here is an analogy: Suppose our society values dancing. The more people dance and the more energetically they dance, the better they are. Now, let's suppose that the most effective way to improve dancing performance is to sting dancers with the venom of tarantulas so they can dance longer and with greater energy. Tarantulas inject venom into victims, which used to be thought of as the cause of "tarantism"—or dancing like crazy to try and shake off the venom.

I don't know if this information about tarantulas is correct. Still, envy is too irritating a mental "poison" to willingly "inject" into our minds merely to get a job done well. I bet most people would prefer to chill and coast rather than purposely feel envious.

This means I don't have to sell you the idea that envy is bad. You probably already know.

This leads us to the next question. How do we deal with envy?

You likely have a sneaky suspicion that it may have something to do with meh.

STEP 1: Watch the impulse. How does it feel inside the head and the body? What sensations does it produce? I feel a burning sensation on the left side of my chest. Watch and take note of whatever you think and feel.

STEP 2: Say *meh* to the feeling (either loudly or mentally, depending on whether you are alone or in company).

STEP 3: Next, ask, "Why am I feeling envious?"

STEP 4: You answer, "Because they have this thing that I want. I have as much right to it as they do. I need it to feel good about myself. I need to feel superior and have self-worth."

STEP 5: Say *meh* to the assumptions. Assumptions are not inherently correct; they must be proven.

STEP 6: After-meh: Play with the assumptions and think more accurately about them.

Life has ups and downs—for everyone. Some of us may have a lot. Others seem to win all the time. No matter. This is not in our control. We can only strive to do our best.

We can beat ourselves and hate others who seem to have it all—this is the reality of envy. But apart from making us miserable, what else does this way of thinking achieve?

A common theme in this book is that, in the face of life's

unproductive, annoying moments, we can get annoyed and frustrated—or we can watch, meh, and move on (or "meh-ve on").

"Meh-ving on" from envy requires a specific mindset. Question the assumption that you need X, Y, or Z. You may need it, but what can you do if you've done your best and failed? *Focus on what you already have.*

Many of us are lucky enough to have our health. So, if you have your health, be grateful for it. Do you have a family? Be grateful. Did you get to eat today? Be grateful. Were you able to take a bath? Brush your teeth? Flush the toilet? Use the bathroom? Walk? Take the stairs?

There are several people, too many people, for whom some or all of these simple, ordinary activities may not be possible. So, if you have any of these, why not be grateful for them? Studies show that being grateful is good for our health—and it feels good as well. A feeling of gratefulness is far more enjoyable than burning with envy. Feelings of gratitude are also more truthful. We have many things that we could easily not have, so it is more honest and smarter to be grateful for them.

Sure, we may not have everything the other guy has, but what about all these other things we do have? You may say, "If I don't have X, I have nothing." But this is incorrect. When we focus on what we lack, we focus on the wrong thing. A small analogy, an unappealing, unappetizing one, might help.

You can smell shit. Or you can smell a rose. Smelling shit is not pleasant. But smelling a rose—unless you have allergies—is much better.

Likewise, when we fixate on the negatives, we are distressed. And when we pay attention to the positives, we fill ourselves with joy. This has been shown by numerous scientists.

To continue with the poop metaphor (with apologies), imagine that your toilet is blocked. You can stare at the poop in the toilet and curse your luck that you have to use the plunger and unblock the toilet. You envy your school friend, who is now a billionaire, with an army of people who unblock the toilets in her house.

You can keep staring at the poop and inhaling (and hating) the noxious aromas that seem to infiltrate into every pore of your body as you wish that you were someone else.

Staring at the poop is equivalent to focusing on the stuff that is not going to fill you with joy. And yet, even in this poop, there is joy. It means you have food to eat—when millions don't. It means your digestion works—when tons of people have constipation or diseases preventing them from using the bathroom. There's a lot to be grateful for.

And let's not forget that you are alive. And that you can see and smell, pick up the plunger, and unblock the toilet. Ask someone who is paralyzed what he would give to be able to walk to the bathroom, stare at some poop, and then use the plunger.

These are all the unappreciated gifts available to you as you stare at crap in a blocked toilet. You can appreciate them. Or you can curse, feel self-pity, and roast in envy. What would you rather have?

Isn't it better to plunge with joy? A clean toilet is a blessing. Millions of people in the world don't have access to clean toilets. How lucky can you get!

And there's another unhelpful solution to envy: envy's mean little cousin, schadenfreude.

TROUBLE 11: SCHADENFREUDE

"Harm-joy." That's what schadenfreude means literally. It is a German word made up of two parts: schaden (harm) and freude (joy).

And so, "harm-joy." But what kind of harm brings joy?

The legendary comedian Mel Brooks says, "Tragedy is when I cut my finger. Comedy is when you fall into an open sewer and die." Similarly, the joy in harm-joy is the joy some of us may feel when someone else suffers harm. Quite often, this someone is somehow "better" or richer or more attractive than us. Someone we envy, someone who is too big for his boots, or someone we think should be brought down a notch (or two—or ten—or thrown into prison).

Schadenfreude has an obvious connection with envy, so I think of it as envy's little cousin. Unlike envy, schadenfreude can feel quite nice. I have to confess that I have enjoyed this feeling whenever I have experienced it. So, what's the problem with it?

There are two problems.

First, it is unkind to feel joy in the suffering of others. I admit that this will not appear to be a problem for some. I know some people want those too full of themselves to fall—and fall hard (and maybe learn from it). Some claim that it is "only human" to feel joy when arrogant people stumble and hurt themselves. I think it might be less than human to do so.

The second problem is one in which we view schadenfreude as a symptom of a disease, not the disease. The disease is dissatisfaction with oneself, leading to the envy of those who have what we don't. Most of us don't feel schadenfreude when a poor person, a refugee, or a down-in-the-dumps homeless man has a humiliating experience. Most people would feel sorry for such a person. No, we feel schadenfreude when someone who is doing very well is humiliated or has a bad experience. This means that schadenfreude is experienced when someone high is brought low. Stemmed from envy or hate, maybe this person is a jerk, they wronged us, or we resent them.

Since envy feeds the feeling of schadenfreude, here is a way to reframe schadenfreude: "I feel schadenfreude because I am envious, and envy is not a great feeling."

Also, observe that if you feel schadenfreude today, you will feel envy tomorrow (or maybe in the next moment) because the disease is still there. We will probably feel envy rather than schadenfreude because there are far too many people we can envy. Statistically speaking, opportunities for feeling schadenfreude will be far fewer.

Seen this way, it makes perfect sense to tackle envy, which will also tackle schadenfreude.

But naturally, these strategies will not wholly eliminate envy, so we will also continue to feel schadenfreude. So, if you feel a flicker of schadenfreude, no worries. It is small potatoes compared to envy. You can rapidly dispose of it. Meh is a quick fix for schadenfreude:

STEP 1: Watch schadenfreude when it arises. How does it feel inside the head and the body? What sensations does it produce? I feel a pleasing glow in the center of my chest and abdomen and a lightness or comfort in my head. Watch and take note of what you think and feel.

STEP 2: Say *meh* to the feeling (either loudly or mentally, depending on whether you are alone or in company).

STEP 3: Next, ask, "Why am I feeling schadenfreude?"

STEP 4: You answer, "Because this person has everything I don't and thinks too much of themselves, and it's nice that they get to suffer. It's not fair that some people have everything and get unfair advantages. If I had what they have, I would have done much better."

STEP 5: You say *meh* to the assumptions. Assumptions are not inherently correct; they must be proven.

STEP 6: After-meh: Play with the assumptions and think more accurately about them.

In this case, accurate thinking is to see schadenfreude in the context of the entire picture. What is it about me that makes me feel this?

This is also an appropriate point to learn about schadenfreude's brilliant opposite (well, sort of): sympathetic joy.

Having meh-ed schadenfreude and its assumptions, we are in a position to try something extremely beneficial.

Sympathetic joy is feeling joy in the happiness of others.

The Dalai Lama did some math and came up with the idea that when we are happy for others, we have a six-billion-to-one chance of being happy (because you can be happy for all the other people in the world). When he said this, there were six billion people on Earth. There are over seven-and-a-half billion people at the time of writing, so the odds are even better.

The idea is that when you hear of the happiness of another, you take pleasure in it and feel happy for them.

I can see what you are thinking. You are thinking that's not realistic, or you will just be faking it. Well, I say, fake it. Faking it is okay because you'll still feel better. Here's my recipe for sympathetic joy, which you can do anytime you want to experience a jolt of happiness:

Think of someone (acquaintance, friend, rival, or celebrity) who has just experienced good fortune and feels happy.

Say to yourself, "That's wonderful! I'm so happy for this person!" It is okay to pretend.

If you find it hard to pretend, put yourself in the person's shoes. Think about how she feels. And then try to feel happy for the person. Like I said, try or pretend, that is to say, fake it. You will eventually make it—to some extent. Maybe not 100 percent, perhaps only 5 percent, but that's still 5 percent happier than you might otherwise be.

This is almost like injecting happiness into yourself. It is better than feeling miserable.

You will feel better. I almost guarantee it.

I am not saying to do this obsessively or to become a sympathetic-joy junkie. But life and media will give you endless opportunities to practice sympathetic joy. You can find real happiness in the many social media posts of your friends. When other people do well and succeed, you will feel better. Imagine that!

And, as you may have figured out, this is also an antidote to envy. Whenever envy strikes you, you can meh, and then when you get to the after-meh, you can turn on the pretend sympathetic joy, and you will feel much better. (Believe me, pretend sympathetic joy rapidly morphs into real sympathetic joy when you begin tasting its many fruits.)

TROUBLE 12: JEALOUSY

Jealousy is a bit like envy, but it is reacting to something that was ours and has been taken by someone else. Or it may mean that we are fearful and anxious that someone else *will* take our place. Typically, jealousy is encountered in romantic situations. But of course, we can be jealous when someone "steals" our friends or "robs" our social status. If you were the top dog in your social circle, and then someone else claims the top-dog spot, you might become jealous of that person. That thing, which was yours, is in someone else's hands now. You can see how jealousy is a bit like envy: We covet what someone else has. The only difference is that you covet what you once used to have.

Like envy, jealousy feels bad—toxic. It can feel horrible to be jealous. You fill up with angry emotions, tension, frustration, and hatred for the person who has taken your spot. You may not be able to stop thinking negative, jealous thoughts. Like envy, jealousy is no picnic. Jealousy can cause sleep loss, anxiety, depression, and loss of appetite. We can apply meh to jealousy:

STEP 1: Watch jealousy when it arises. How does it feel inside the head and the body? What sensations does it produce? I remember being jealous when I was a teenager. I felt anxiety and palpitations. It was terrible. I vowed never to feel this way again. Thankfully, I haven't. Simply note whatever it is you feel.

STEP 2: Say *meh* to the feeling (either loudly or mentally, depending on whether you are alone or in company).

STEP 3: Next, ask, "Why am I feeling jealous?"

STEP 4: You answer, "Because this person has taken what belongs to me. I will go to pieces if I lose this."

STEP 5: Say *meh* to the assumptions. Assumptions are not inherently correct; they must be proven.

STEP 6: After-meh: Play with the assumptions and think more accurately about them.

The two assumptions behind the other assumptions are 1. something belongs to me, and 2. I can't survive without it.

Are these true?

First and foremost, *absolutely nothing belongs to us*. Nothing. We came into this world after being nothing and popped up on the scene one day. There is no "we" (apart from the raw materials that form us, which we don't own). So, the first assumption is incorrect. Even things like our health, wealth, and mental resources depend on external things. Take them away, and we lose these things. Take away the raw materials forming us, and we don't exist.

The second assumption takes the first one for granted. Since nothing belongs to us, there is no question of surviving without this something-that-doesn't-actually-belong-to-us.

We have been given gifts: the gifts of life and mental and physical things we seem to own (but we could think we are leasing them temporarily). I am not suggesting that we should let anarchy rule or grab what doesn't belong to us. Nothing belongs to us, so grabbing is out of the question—we'd be grabbing what's not ours (nothing is), which is wrong. We can't walk into someone's house and take something, saying, "Well, nothing belongs to anyone, so I can take anything I want." This argument is wrong, and it can (and should) land us in prison.

The way society is formatted, we are like stewards or custodians of our lives and our possessions. But if circumstances change—let's suppose there is a flood or earthquake, the stock market crashes, we lose our jobs, or we have a heart attack or stroke—well, we stop being custodians at that point, and other people take over.

We can't use the term "jealousy" to describe something taken away from us criminally. If it is a crime, we are dealing with a different situation. We feel jealous when we think what's ours is no longer ours (excluding theft). We don't own the affections and friendships of others any more than we own the amount of oxygen in the air.

The correct way of looking at this is to recognize that nothing—zero—is ours. At most, we have squatting rights. And when it comes to other people and how they feel about us, we don't even have squatting rights. There is no rule saying that we should be loved, that a spouse must love another spouse, or that someone should perpetually remain the most popular in their social circle.

These gifts may remain with us, or they may not. Thinking they are ours is a mistake. Once we correct this mistake, we may feel a twinge of jealousy, but we can quickly meh it, meh the assumptions, and move into a jealousy-free after-meh life.

TROUBLE 13: ANGER/WRATH/HOSTILITY

Nanny mental state *I* wants X. Nanny mental state *I* doesn't get

X (someone or something may be standing in the way). Nanny mental state *I* gets hopping mad.

This is anger in a nutshell. Anger, wrath, rage, hostility—these are shades of the same process, to varying degrees. Wrath is out of control, high-amplitude anger.

Because we are human, we get angry. Whenever we don't get what we want, we have the potential to get angry. When someone crosses or double-crosses us, we can get angry. We can feel hostility toward certain individuals. When the provocation feels extreme, the anger may also be extreme—wrath, which some people equate with anger plus action, violent action.

Anger is an explosive emotion, and while we are in its grip, we may be swept away, overpowered by it. We may act unpredictably, violently, aggressively, forcefully, or cruelly. It is no surprise that wrath is considered one of the seven deadly sins. It can turn deadly. A raging, wrathful person may kill another. We all know about cases where rage, for example, road rage, can cause an enraged person to kill someone.

In extreme cases, anger can also kill the person feeling the anger. Outbursts of anger may, in a small percentage of cases, lead to death from heart attacks. So, anger can literally, physically kill the angry person. No wonder that Professor Redford Williams has written a book called *Anger Kills*.

Over the long term, anger and hostility are related to a bunch of health effects: early death, heart attack, hypertension, heart disease, strokes, abdominal pain, anxiety, asthma, depression, eczema, headache, insomnia, etc.

Plus, angry, hostile people don't make friends easily, or others may avoid them. So they miss out on social support. Lack of social support, too, has been linked to early death.

Anger is thus a very harmful emotion and is best stopped before it becomes overpowering. If it can be avoided altogether (it can, in some cases), that is even better.

Fortunately, it is possible to rapidly stem the tide of anger through various strategies. Here is one of them:

STEP 1: Watch anger when it arises. How does it feel inside the head and the body? What sensations does it produce? For me, it feels like a "rising hot column" inside my head. Watch and take note of whatever you think and feel.

STEP 2: You say *meh* to the feeling (either loudly or mentally, depending on whether you are alone or in company).

STEP 3: Next, ask, "Why am I feeling anger/wrath/hostility?"

STEP 4: You answer, "The things said or done were awful. It robbed me of my rights. Nobody should do or say those kinds of things."

STEP 5: Say *meh* to the assumptions. Assumptions are not inherently correct; they must be proven.

STEP 6: After-meh: Play with the assumptions and think more accurately about them.

In the after-meh phase, you are ready to do something about anger because you know it is a harmful emotion. Is any provocation sufficient to make you want to harm yourself? Most people would probably say no.

The assumptions that anger depends on are all rooted in the nanny mental state that demands that *I* gets what it wants. But this nanny mental state, like all nanny mental states, is a wispy, wimpy, ephemeral neurochemical activity in the brain. Later on, when you are past anger, you may feel like kicking yourself for letting yourself get carried away by your anger. *If only*, you might think, *I had kept my mouth shut.*

Luckily, we can easily take care of the assumptions on which anger rests.

Assumption 1: *The things said or done were awful.* Perhaps they are. Awful things happen in the world too often, unfortunately. But the cold, hard fact is that neither we nor the things (awful or nice) are in control. Let me elaborate with an example.

Imagine an annoying fly coming to rest on your nose. You have a hammer in your hand. You can bring it smashing down on your nose in anger. Naturally, the fly is adept at dodging hammers, so it will quickly fly away. Your nose, however, will not be so lucky. You may break your nose with the hammer. Would you smash your nose because you are mad at the fly?

A bout of anger is as helpful as breaking your nose. You are probably not going to change anything. All you will manage to do is make the situation worse. And, if you are the sort who is easily angered, you are harming yourself over the long run (given the laundry list of diseases associated with anger and hostility).

Assumption 2: *It robbed me of my rights.*

Yes, as human beings, we have certain inalienable rights. That is true. We should be able to live our lives without being harmed by others. We should be able to express our opinions and protect ourselves. But does it make sense to get one of a long list of mental and physical problems or worsen the situation? If we want to protect our rights, wouldn't it be smarter to figure out a creative or intelligent way to do so? Do we have to shatter our noses in the process? Is there a better way of dealing with a fly problem?

Even if there isn't a better solution to deal with "flies" in our lives, it still doesn't make sense to harm ourselves with hard or impossible-to-control anger.

Assumption 3: *Nobody should do or say those kinds of things.*

Unless the things being done are criminal acts, we can't stop people from doing or saying things, even if they are wretched and ignoble. An awful person saying or doing a terrible thing is the same as a stupid computer or TV acting up. They are equally "within their rights" to act in the annoying way they "want" to. A computer "can't help" freezing or functioning annoyingly, right? Just as the awful person is who they are because of their experiences.

These are the many "flies" that plague our existence. There may be nothing we can do about them. But it is illogical to react with something—anger, rage, hostility, wrath—that will only end up causing us harm.

We did many stupid, unhelpful things when we were little, but we don't do these things as adults. In the same way, anger, which may seem "natural" or an "I can't help it" type of response, can yield when we see its stupidity. There is no need to suppress anger when you can let it whimper away on its own, by shrugging it off and saying *meh*.

A Word About Hate

Hate is the result of anger, envy, jealousy, pride, dissatisfaction, or injustice. You can hate a person, an animal, a thing, or a circumstance. I have not discussed hate separately because if you deal with the causes of hate, then you deal with hate.

For example, if you hate a former friend who has betrayed you, you may feel a mix of anger, envy, or injustice. But if you deal with all the emotions that go into creating a feeling of hate, then you will find that hate itself has gone.

It's a bit like the story of the boy who takes apart a fly and then gets puzzled because he can't find the fly anymore. Once the fly has been separated into its many parts, no fly is left. Hate is like that. It is built on the backs of negative emotions and opinions. Once these are removed, hate is also removed.

TROUBLE 14: WORRY

Worry is one of those things that may be impossible to shake off. Suppose I am worried about X. Here's how the shaking-off attempt typically works: I am worried about X. I say to myself (or someone says to me), "Don't be worried about X—it is of no use." I know that, but I can't shake it off.

Worry is a bit like dental plaque in this sense. Always there, stuck to the back of your teeth, jumping up and down. But you can't get rid of it completely.

The usual advice about worry can be given in four lines:

LINE 1: There are things you can change and things you can't.

LINE 2: Change what you can.

LINE 3: What you can't change, there's no point in worrying about.

LINE 4: So don't worry about it.

This advice is good, but it has a small problem. It can be hard to put into practice.

In my case, I do wonderfully well with lines 1, 2, and 3. But somehow, I flounder and flail when I get to line 4.

The reason is that you can't stop worrying simply by telling yourself not to worry. It can actually create a lot of anxiety because it seems like this advice makes a lot of sense (it does), but then when you try to apply it, it doesn't work the way you want it to. And that frustrates you and causes tension and anxiety. You want it to work, but it doesn't.

It's as if you had convinced yourself that you could and should teach your cat to speak Spanish. Teaching a cat to speak Spanish may be as effective as telling yourself not to worry, no matter how logical the reason.

Just because lines 1 to 3, in the traditional recipe for not worrying, make perfect sense doesn't mean we can easily leap to line 4.

The late Dr. Daniel Wegner said that if you try not to think about a polar bear, you will be unable to stop thinking of a polar bear. Worry is a bit like that.

Another strategy is required. And this other strategy is—well, you know, right?

STEP 1: Watch worry when it arises. How does it feel inside the head and the body? What sensations does it produce? I feel a "knot" in the center of my forehead and an unpleasant burning sensation in my chest and abdomen. Watch and take note of whatever you think and feel.

STEP 2: Say *meh* to the feeling (either loudly or mentally, depending on whether you are alone or in company).

STEP 3: Next, ask, "Why am I feeling worry?"

STEP 4: You answer, "Because things might go wrong or not work out. That would be a total disaster. I will decompensate if things go wrong."

STEP 5: Say *meh* to these assumptions. Assumptions are not inherently correct; they must be proven.

STEP 6: After-meh: Play with the assumptions and think more accurately about them.

Our worry assumptions are based on the premise that something terrible will happen in the future. Our job is to find out if this is true or if it matters.

Humans are pretty adaptive. In other words, when things happen, good or bad, we adjust and adapt to them rapidly and return to our baseline level of being. People who undergo tragedies or difficulties can be broken by them, but they often manage to get past them and get over them. So, our assumption that "if this happens, I will lose it completely" may be true in the short run but not in the long run.

No matter what we do, things will not stay peachy and rosy

forever. We will suffer setbacks at some point in time. We can be healthy for a very long time if we are lucky, but no matter how healthy we are, we won't live forever.

So, if you are worried about things going wrong, the sad truth is that things will eventually go wrong or not stay perfect. That's just the way life is. But the assumption about our reaction is incorrect. We will manage somehow, no matter what happens.

This is a very liberating thought. Just a day ago, I was very worried about something bad happening, how it would feel, and what I would do. But then I remembered the times I went through stuff I would have preferred to avoid. In all these, I managed just fine. So I said meh to my assumption and realized that it could get plenty unpleasant, but somehow, I am sure I will be able to muddle through.

I want to share a story. I have found it to be very amusing and helpful.

This man is about to have a tax audit. He goes to his spiritual adviser and says, "Should I wear my best suit to show how serious I am about cooperating with the audit? Or should I wear tattered clothes to show how poor I am, that I don't have the kind of money the tax auditors think I have?" The spiritual adviser sighs and says, "My son, this reminds me of this woman getting married. She asks her mother, 'Mom, do I spend my savings on the most expensive, amazing wedding dress, or do I save the money and buy a cheap but okay dress from the outlet mall?' And the mother says, "My dear daughter, it is my experience that no matter what you wear, you are going to get screwed." (In the version I heard, another word for "screwed" was used, but I want to keep it clean.)

"What you wear" is the equivalent of the mental attitude or nanny mental state of worry. It is being concerned with the outcome when we all know the outcome is, well, not one in which we live happily ever after. Life has no "happily ever after," since life ends.

The nanny mental state of "no matter what you wear, you are going to get screwed" is the devil may care (almost), or meh state. I suppose a small percentage of the things we worry about will come to pass, but so what? That's just the way it is. If you are perpetually worried that you might die today—well, one day, you will be right!

We now know how to counteract the assumption that makes us dread what will happen *if* something else happens. We counteract it by using our own experiences in life. Each of us has been through good times and bad, all of which are memories. Luckily, most of us are not as disturbed by our memory of disturbing events as we were when these events happened. This shows that *if* something we worry about might happen, we will get through it somehow. It may be dreadful, but it likely won't last forever. And we will hopefully come out on the other side of it. Or we won't. Big deal! Meh! (This obviously doesn't apply to those who suffer from PTSD or trauma survivors who may need professional help.)

TROUBLE 15: WHEN LIFE SEEMS UNFAIR

Why do good things happen to bad people, and why do bad things happen to good people? Why do some people have a string of misfortunes while others have endless streaks of good luck?

I am not the only one who has wondered why life seems unfair. I am grateful for all that I have, but at the same time, I feel it is unfair that I don't have X, Y, or Z.

No one—or almost no one—can move through life without some unfairness.

When we perceive life as unfair, we may do the following: become depressed, pessimistic, or anxious; start despairing; become greedy; become envious; become furious; go to extreme lengths, including violence, to tip the balance in our favor and make things "fair."

We can try and meh this feeling:

STEP 1: Watch the feeling when it arises. How does it feel inside the head and the body? What sensations does it produce? Watch and take note of whatever you think and feel.

STEP 2: You say *meh* to the feeling (either loudly or mentally, depending on whether you are alone or in company).

STEP 3: Next, ask, "Why am I feeling that life is unfair?"

STEP 4: You answer, "Because nothing good ever happens to me. Why am I always so unlucky? Everyone should have equal luck, opportunities, and advantages, a fair playing field."

STEP 5: You say *meh* to this assumption. Assumptions are not inherently correct; they must be proven.

STEP 6: After-meh: Play with the assumptions and think more accurately about them.

What would be a more helpful way of thinking about this question of unfairness?

Warren Buffett, one of the wealthiest humans on Earth, reportedly told his children they had won the "ovarian lottery." This is both amusing and truthful. None of us has chosen to be here, and we owe our existence to a combination of factors. We are where we are, and that is just the way life is. The person born disabled and the person born with every advantage both have zero control over their stations in life. They can each make heroic efforts and achieve many things, but even these depend upon them having mental and physical qualities—which they didn't construct on their own. We depend on something other than "us" for everything. And I mean *everything*.

So, the truth of the situation is that we are "borrowed"

creatures. When we think that life is unfair, what we are saying is "A nanny mental state makes me think life is unfair."

But remember, this nanny mental state is "borrowed." It is borrowed from things outside of itself. For this (or any) nanny mental state to exist, there must be a living body and a brain, both of which "we" do not provide. Our bodies function until they don't, and our brains are endowed with a certain amount of brainpower. They are, essentially, "on loan."

So, if we are here on Earth and think that life is unfair, it is a bit ironic. We are using the brain to think this thought, a brain we might never have had. Here's an analogy.

It's as if I popped up suddenly with a tiny piece of chocolate, and I saw someone else surrounded by a sea of cakes. I could say life is unfair. But is it? Can we legitimately complain about unfairness when the person who got the cakes got them as a "gift," and my tiny piece of chocolate is also a gift? Both of us could have had nothing (or not existed). Should we be arguing about gifts?

We can complain about anything we want, but our complaint doesn't make much sense in this case. To understand why, ask, "Who am I complaining to?" The answer can be one of two:

If you believe in God, you can certainly complain to God, but God's answer (based on thousands of years of religious thought) might be something like this: "You don't know what you're talking about. You wouldn't even be here if it weren't for Me. Your life, your everything, is not your own. Since I know more than you about everything, your judgment about unfairness is incorrect. I know what's correct and the way things should be. It's like two beggars arguing about what they get from a king when neither of them would have anything if the king didn't give them something. You can't argue that someone giving you a gift is unfair." This is just a guess on my part. Of course, I have no idea what God would say. But most religions understand and believe that God knows more than we do and that part of being religious is to accept God's judgments and gifts without thinking they are "unfair."

If you don't believe in God, then you probably think you're here just because you are, as a result of random processes. Forces came together, and after many billions of years, you appeared on the scene. From this way of thinking, your position in life results from forces acting over countless millennia. So, to whom can you legitimately complain? If everything is the result of chance and randomness, then if you complain about life's unfairness, what's the point? Who is listening to you, and who can change things for you? Even your thoughts are (from this kind of reasoning) the result of random forces, so why pay any attention to them? You might as well argue that it's not fair there are two hydrogens and one oxygen in water, whereas there is one sodium and one chloride in salt. Why can't these forces be fair and make water and salt the "same" or equal? Or why are cockroaches considered disgusting and cats cute? Why can't cockroaches and cats be the same or equal?

Reasoning in this way can make "unfairness" more manageable and easier to handle because we can easily see the absurdity of our thoughts. But some of you may disagree. If you do, then try meh-ditation and move on to something else. The way our minds are, we can easily slip into other thoughts and other concerns.

After you have meh-ed the feeling of unfairness away, I'd like to recommend two things: gratitude (previously discussed) and helping others. Too many people have too many problems. Focusing on other people's problems and helping them has many advantages. First, it helps others. Second, it distracts you from your own problems. I knew this guy who was facing a severe crisis. He asked his son's friend for help. The son's friend said, "I really can't help at this time because, as you know, my wife just died of metastatic cancer, and I have our young child to look after." This guy said, "Don't worry about your problems. Worry about my problems instead." He may have been self-centered, but he had a point. Worrying about other people's problems can take your mind off your own. So, if you feel down about life's unfairness, how about helping someone who needs a helping hand?

TROUBLE 16: WHEN THINGS DON'T GO OUR WAY—DISSATISFACTION WITH LIFE

Welcome to the world!

Things not going our way and being dissatisfied are the overarching themes of a large chunk of economics, politics, religion, commerce, philosophy, and, of course, the self-help publishing industry, of which this book is a tiny example.

If everything always went our way, we might wonder if we had died and gone to paradise!

It's like the story of Buddha. Buddha was shielded from all pain and suffering for the initial part of his life. But he managed to stumble upon people in pain and suffering by chance. This threw him into a psychological and spiritual crisis. And this led, eventually, to the four noble truths. The first of these truths was *dukkha*. This word means suffering, pain, dissatisfaction, and misery. Which essentially summarizes a large chunk of our lives.

Though you may try hard, you may not escape from the fangs of dissatisfaction. Things will never, ever go one-hundred-percent your way. This is a fact.

Therefore, it behooves us to try to find a solution for it. The major religions and philosophies do a marvelous job of presenting us with superb strategies for dealing with dukkha. Meh can also help. My recommendation is to continue practicing your religion or philosophy. And you can occasionally add meh to help reorient you to the truths of your way of life.

STEP 1: Watch the feeling of dissatisfaction when it arises.

How does it feel inside the head and the body? What sensations does it produce? I feel an unpleasant knot in my forehead, a bit like a tension headache. Watch and take note of whatever you think and feel.

STEP 2: You say *meh* to the feeling (either loudly or mentally, depending on whether you are alone or in company).

STEP 3: Next, ask, "Why am I feeling dissatisfied?"

STEP 4: You answer, "Because I don't have X. If I did, I would be satisfied."

STEP 5: Say *meh* to this assumption. Assumptions are not inherently correct; they must be proven.

STEP 6: After-meh: Play with the assumptions and think more accurately about them.

We have already seen that we will want something else once we get X. It's just how we are wired. We get a dopamine rush from something, but then we want more of that or something else because we're bored with the first something, and so on.

You could say we are addicted to wanting something—either more of something or a different something. It's a fact that we will never be permanently satisfied with anything. We literally can't. We aren't biologically able to be satisfied forever. This is why we are stuck on the hedonic treadmill, where we keep wanting more and more.

A more realistic understanding of dissatisfaction is that we are stuck with it.

Most of us spend a lot of time avoiding the 4 Ds: disease, distress, discomfort, and death. All of these add up to an overall biggie: dissatisfaction with our lot in life. For most of us, escape might be difficult or impossible. These Ds will hunt us down, and we will succumb to them. If not now, then later;

if not later, then even later; if not even later, then eventually. When I see some young people, I notice they are full of life and hopeful. That's wonderful—I am not complaining about it. But many seem oblivious to the eventual fate that awaits them, which may be a good thing—I don't wish them to be depressed out of their minds! But at the same time, I think it is better to be prepared for what may befall us. Some of them will learn this fate sooner than others. We feel sorry for such young ones who discover the harshness of life too soon. We say that their youth has been snatched away. I think this way too. But truthfully, objectively, this falls into the "life is unfair" complaint.

Life denies us complete security. Life ends in death, and there is nothing we can do about it. Recall the story of the meatballs. Meatballs may revel in being meatballs, but their purpose is to be eaten, un-meatball-ed, broken into little bits, denied the glue that maintains their meatball shape.

This is a good thing to remember. It can keep us from getting too ahead of ourselves, of thinking we are the be-all and end-all, that we are more important than we are. Yes, we may hopefully accomplish great things, but we must never forget that we are human meatballs too.

But I don't want to be the bearer of doom and gloom, to be a Diwan Downer about all this unwelcome information (which everybody knows and nearly everybody ignores in their daily lives). It's tough to strike a cheerful note when contemplating the grisly end that awaits you. And yet, strangely enough, there is a great joy in it too. After-meh allows us to combat dissatisfaction with the realization of our ultimate destruction.

How?

First, next time you are dissatisfied about something, reflect that, thankfully, one day, it will all end, and you won't have to worry about any earthly concern, no matter how important it may seem to you now. It's a liberation that awaits us. I recall a delightful saying by Idries Shah: "When the house catches fire, the toothache flies out of the window."[14]

In the present context, the toothache is dissatisfaction.

The fire is the realization, the fact of our destruction.

Dissatisfaction is a minor complaint compared to the thought of annihilation. A pithy way of remembering this is to use a simple phrase, such as "Dissatisfied? Don't worry, you'll be dead soon enough."

Second, faced with our destruction, which is liberation from earthly domination, we can focus better on what is important. Dissatisfaction will flee in the face of our reflection of our final demise. It will help us devote our energies to what is useful: being helpful to others, being kind and compassionate, or being as useful as you can be to others—and yourself. Remember, when you are not worrying about yourself, many of your "important" concerns, angst, and anxieties will disappear. You may find yourself happier.

There is a line, I believe, that leads from dissatisfaction to happiness. It crosses over the swamp of unpleasant facts about our destruction.

It's a bit like being on your deathbed. People say that when we are on deathbeds, many of the things that matter today will seem completely unimportant. The things that do seem to matter include the following:

1. The wish that we had the courage to lead a life that was true to ourselves, not one that was expected of us.

2. The wish that we had worked less hard and taken it easier.

3. The wish that we had the courage to express what we really felt.

---

14   Shah, Idries, 2020, *A Perfumed Scorpion*. ISF Publishing. Kindle.

4. The wish that we had kept in touch with our friends.

5. The wish that we had allowed ourselves to be happier.[15]

All these wishes express a desire to move us away from the little island of *I*—an *I* that keeps us from being happier, friendlier, more relaxed, more chilled out, and more in touch with our deeper feelings of being true to ourselves.

The solution, of course, is to laugh in the face of dissatisfaction, say *meh*, and think pleasantly about your demise. Be on your deathbed today, so you hopefully won't have any regrets later when it is your time to go. And an added plus is that you'll be able to do some good.

Many years ago, I wrote an idiotic little novel called *My Hemorrhoid—a Man, his Hemorrhoid, his Destiny*. The whole idea was that the hero, a wimpy, spineless creature, was fixated on his hemorrhoid and was thus finding it difficult to do the right thing (saving the world, in this case). This is what I am saying here. We have to get past our dissatisfaction through any method we can (including the one I have given here) to do our bit to help things along. We may not save the world, but how about saving the tiniest part of it—the one you have the smallest bit of control over?

TROUBLE 17: BOREDOM

Boredom may be thought of as baby dissatisfaction. Here, we are not dissatisfied in a big way with our lives. Instead, we find ourselves dissatisfied, with nothing worthwhile to do or stimulate us.

Boredom happens when life seems to lack color. It may feel empty of any meaning or purpose. We may reach out for some action, anything that can relieve us of the tedium, the dullness of the moment.

---

15 Ware, Bronnie, 2019. *The Top Five Regrets of the Dying*. Hay House. Kindle.

What it boils down to is that we are not being stimulated enough. There is not enough there to entertain, amuse, or engage us in a way we value.

For example, a security guard may fall asleep with boredom. It's always the same drill. People walk past with the correct identification or badge, and the security guard lets them through. Or, if they lack the appropriate badge, the guard may question them. The process can be repetitive and boring.

Everyone can relate to instances—waiting in an office, airport, plane, etc.—when time doesn't move fast enough.

The degree of mental pain or anguish can be a lot, and studies have shown that some people prefer a small but slightly painful electric shock to being bored. When left on their own without anything to do, some subjects in a study pressed a button they knew would shock them *because they were bored.*

Talk about literally stimulating yourself, unpleasantly, rather than being bored. Blaise Pascal would have understood. He wrote, "All of humanity's problems stem from man's inability to sit quietly in a room alone."

If people prefer actual physical pain to boredom, what else might they do when bored? I hope my fears are exaggerated, but I suspect they are not. People do all kinds of things all the time, and some of them are terrible. I imagine that some people do these things because they are bored. If they had a good book to read or something interesting to do, it is possible, isn't it, that they might not do the terrible thing? It seems likely that the influence of boredom may cause recreational drug usage and some percentage of crimes.

It has been shown that boredom is linked to anger, aggression, impulsive behavior, gambling, and other negative behaviors.

Doing poorly at school, depression, anxiety, poor job performance, and not having a sense of purpose in life are also associated with boredom.

So, there is a price to pay for boredom.

Here is how we can apply meh and after-meh to boredom:

STEP 1: Watch the feeling of boredom when it arises. How does it feel inside the head and the body? What sensations does it produce? I simply feel that there's no point in anything, and nothing seems interesting. Watch and take note of whatever you think and feel.

STEP 2: You say *meh* to the feeling (either loudly or mentally, depending on whether you are alone or in company).

STEP 3: Next, ask, "Why am I feeling bored?"

STEP 4: You answer, "Because nothing seems interesting or worth doing. If I had something valuable or interesting to do, I wouldn't feel bored."

STEP 5: You say *meh* to this assumption. Assumptions are not inherently correct; they must be proven.

STEP 6: After-meh: Play with the assumptions and think more accurately about them.

The assumption is correct because there may be nothing valuable or interesting to do.

But, it is *more accurate* to say that there may be nothing *that seems* valuable or interesting to do. And the lack of anything valuable or interesting translates into a lack of stimulation for us—something to keep us entertained and engaged.

"*Seems like*" implies a perception problem. We conclude incorrectly that *because it* seems like *there is nothing valuable or interesting, there is nothing valuable or interesting*.

But there might be something valuable and/or interesting. When we are bored, it is possible that we are not catching on to the interesting aspects.

How might we find value or interest in a moment or long stretches of seemingly meaningless moments?

Here's one way to go about it: We can observe the moment or some aspect of the moment in great detail. For example, waiting at the airport can be a mind-numbingly boring business. But there are activities bustling around you.

You can people-watch. People are running about to and fro, some bored, some anxious, some in a hurry, some frustrated, some angry, some belligerent. You can think about the human situation, empathize, put yourself in their situation, and wonder, *This is what life is like, what we are like; this is us, not just at airports but everywhere in life.* Some of us may wonder, *Is there any other way of being—a calmer, more joyful, more fulfilling way of being?* This may lead to curiosity. If there's one, we may go to an airport bookstore or check on our phones for insights from psychology about anxiety, anger, frustration, or some other topic inspired by what we get to see when we people-watch. Airports are almost like laboratories where a wide spectrum of human behavior is on display.

You can insect-watch. Insects are everywhere, and some may be intrigued by them. Maybe an ant or spider is determinedly making its way from A to B. If you are an insect person, you may have wondered about the amazing way such small creatures go about their business. You may have thought, *How tiny are their brains or intestines?* Or some other fascinating aspect about insects.

You can floor-watch. I am using this as an example of how even a "boring" floor can become interesting. Many airport floors have dull, uninspiring, and lackluster carpets. But take a look at that carpet. I am not suggesting you get on all fours and start peering intently at it—this might invite unwelcome attention from worried passengers and airport officials who might think you've lost it. No, just gaze at the floor. All matter, including boring carpets, is made up of atoms, and atoms are mostly empty space. I am not a physicist, but I think I am correct when I say that all solid things—even the hardest ones—are mostly empty space at the atomic level. Isn't that amazing? One can gaze at a carpet, a boring one, in complete awe of its mostly empty atomic structure. You might even ask, "What's an empty space like you doing in a dull carpet like this?"

I guess I am saying that even the dullest, most boring moments are packed with interesting things—people, other creatures, objects, air, space, and so on. Any of these can individually provoke awe and amazement. Our life on Earth is filled with awe-inspiring elements. Next time you get bored, look at your nails or think about how your stomach is secreting acid. We are a hive of cells, buzzing with the most intricate, extraordinary cellular activity.

If we put our minds to it, there is a lot to wonder about, and wonder can drive out boredom.

PROCRASTINATION OF THE BORING KIND

I want to spend just a moment on this. I mentioned that we procrastinate on some tasks because they appear boring. The method I have given above should work for that. Take whatever task you have (say, filling out a tedious form or working on a dull project). As you do, reflect on the objects, the papers, you, the room around you. As I have shown above, everything is full of wonders when viewed at the atomic or subatomic scale. Use this strategy to turn dull tasks into something fun, enjoyable, or awe-inspiring. Next time I gather documents to give to my accountant for my taxes, I will appreciate that my ability to email documents to my accountant depends on my accountant being there, me being here, and there being such things as computers and the internet and billions of years of history that have led to all of us being brought together in this way. Emailing can become like an ode to the joy of being alive, being around, and being able to do these sorts of things.

In every moment, including boring ones, you are still there. Get curious, think deeply, and gawk with awe at the amazing aspects of life, including all of existence: nature, you, other people, inanimate objects, other species, the air we breathe, mountains, rivers, everything.

Awe, wonder, curiosity—they can rekindle interest. Invite these and watch boredom flee.

And remember, you can always recall your purpose. Bored people, it has been shown, lack a sense of purpose. They are adrift. Lost. So, remembering your purpose can attack this aspect of boredom.

Do you have a purpose? When you are bored, you may think that you have no purpose or that nothing has a purpose. But there is a purpose. All of us have a purpose. If you need a reminder, look no further than the next section.

TROUBLE 18: WHEN YOU THINK YOU OR YOUR LIFE HAS NO PURPOSE

Every so often, when we get bored, stressed, or hopeless in the face of too many things to do, we may ask ourselves, "What's the point? What does it all mean?"

Or we may conclude that we and our lives have no meaning.

Not so fast, though. Here is a situation that is perfect for the meh recipe.

STEP 1: Watch the feeling of purposelessness when it arises. How does it feel inside the head and the body? What sensations does it produce? I feel sad and dispirited. Sometimes, there is a hollow feeling in my chest and abdomen. Watch and take note of thoughts and feelings.

STEP 2: You say *meh* to the feeling (either loudly or mentally, depending on whether you are alone or in company).

STEP 3: Next, ask, "Why am I feeling that my life has no purpose?"

STEP 4: You answer, "Because I don't feel that what I am doing has meaning or value. I wish I could do something meaningful instead of this nonsense. Everything is pointless in the end because we will all die eventually. I feel empty inside."

STEP 5: You say *meh* to these assumptions. Assumptions are not inherently correct; they must be proven.

STEP 6: After-meh: Play with the assumptions and think more accurately about them.

Are any of these assumptions valid? Is life really like Shakespeare said: "a tale told by an idiot, full of sound and fury, signifying nothing"? Some context may be helpful. The character who thinks life is a tale told by an idiot has committed several murders, urged by his ambition to get ahead and the insistence of his equally evil wife. He and his wife are awful people who have committed atrocities to get ahead in life. They have indeed behaved like idiots—evil idiots.

Such a person is justified in thinking that life is pointless, idiotic, and meaningless. This person has spent his time on Earth being corrupt and murderous. He is filled with negativity and corruption. Is it any surprise that he should wonder if there is any more to life than all this awfulness—awfulness created by himself?

If we engage in evil, all we can see is evil. Our nanny mental states faithfully portray the dominant thoughts in our minds. If we behave kindly, we feel better because our nanny mental states are kinder and more beneficial. To behave badly, we must feel bad. If we felt kind and compassionate, would we be running around murdering people or being obnoxious?

It's as if we were hell-bent on running into brick walls at full speed, and then when we felt pain, we said to ourselves, "What's the point of it all?" It's all so nonsensical and idiotic.

If, before we run into the wall one more time, we take a moment and think to ourselves, *Hey, what are you doing?* we might stop and answer, *I am about to run at top speed into that wall over there.* And we might then ask, reasonably, *That seems like a fairly stupid thing to do. Any reason why you are doing this?* And we might decide that, on balance, it's not the smartest thing in the world to smash headlong into a wall.

And we might stop doing that.

The analogy is extreme, but I want to make a point. Thoughtlessly doing activities can distance us from our purpose and our meaning. We may not see any value in what we are doing.

So, lack of purpose or, more appropriately, *feeling* a lack of purpose can be a temporary or permanent feeling if we do things thoughtlessly, without understanding or paying attention to what we are doing. If these things are harmful, bad, or evil, we should think hard about whether this is what we want to do. If we continue doing bad things, then we deserve what we get.

(I will operate under the assumption that you are not doing horrible things.)

Suppose you are caught in the rat race, doing multiple jobs or juggling numerous responsibilities. It's possible to get overwhelmed, fling your arms in despair, and yell, "It's all so meaningless! My life is absurd! What's the point of it all?"

But if thoughtlessness is connected to a sense of meaninglessness, then we may be close to a solution. What if the answer was a little bit of thoughtfulness?

By thoughtfulness, I mean something like mindfulness or observing what you are doing and asking yourself what you are doing.

Here is a simple recipe for what to do when you are feeling a lack of purpose.

In the after-meh phase, you

1. Stop for a moment and ask yourself, "What are you doing?"
2. You answer, "I am doing this and that . . . and so on."
3. You ask, "How do you feel about this?"
4. You answer, "How do you think I feel? Like crap. I feel like none of these things matter, or they all matter, that I don't matter, that this madness is pointless and never ends."
5. You say, "Okay, well, meh. What you need to do is see that you are reacting to all this craziness. And remember your purpose. What is your life's purpose? Do you remember?"
6. And then you remind yourself of your life's purpose.

The purpose could be different for different people. It could be religion. It could be general kindness. Or maybe you just want to get things done and not be a jerk.

All these are purposes. Goals.

When you feel like life has no purpose, all you have to do is take a moment, ask yourself what's up, and remind yourself of your purpose. Then, you could say to yourself, "Yes, I am doing these million and one things, all driving me crazy. But there is a point. My life's purpose is X. The things I am doing now may not seem to have a connection with X, but they do. If I don't do these things, life will become chaotic, and I will not be able to do the things that matter to me—the things that are my life's goal. It's like doing laundry. If I let the dirty clothes pile up, the conditions in my life might become unbearable. Doing laundry may not seem worthy, and it is a bit of a pain, but keeping order in my life helps me achieve my purpose. So, laundry is an essential part of my life's purpose. In the same way, my tough jobs, responsibilities, and so on are connected to my life's purpose."

Inject some sweetness into your life. How?

Be kind.

That's it. It's nothing earthshaking.

Imagine you are stuck in a situation that makes you question your life's purpose. It could be an endless queue at an office, grocery store, or elsewhere. It could be doing something you have no interest in but are forced to do. You can say to yourself, "Yes, I am stuck here, but I am going to be kind to others and pleasant, helpful, and cooperative."

We have control over *how* we do what we have to do. We can frown and do what must be done. Or we can smile and do what we have to. If something has to be done, and there's no getting out of it, why not have a pleasant attitude? Kindness and pleasantness sweeten the mental landscape.

What I am suggesting is not impossible. All it takes is a little bit of practice.

PART 4

MEH AND THE GOOD STUFF

WHY DO WE WATCH?

There is a common theme in using the power of meh to reclaim our lives.

It all begins with watching.

What happens when we watch?

Suppose that a particular part of the brain, let's call it part A, is involved with a certain nanny mental state. When I am mad, a particular bunch of nerve cells (neurons) might be firing off. When I am jealous, it might be another collection of neurons doing their thing. Another set may be active when I am bored, and so on. The idea is that our mental states correspond to activity within certain neurons.

Now consider what happens when we pay attention or take note, that is to say, carefully watch what is happening inside us. First, we may notice thoughts or feelings. We may further feel something in our bodies. It could be anything: a sensation of burning, churning, or yearning, a knot somewhere, a feeling of tightness, tension, an ache, etc.

When we watch, another, *different* group of neurons is

brought into play. So immediately, the action has moved from spot A (original thoughts/feelings) to spot B (the place where we are watching them) in the brain.

This means that our focus has shifted from feeling something to watching us feel something.

Why is this important?

The most obvious reason is that when we feel a certain way, it corresponds to neurons in a part of the brain. But when we shift to a different bunch of *watching* neurons, we are obviously no longer in the same part that is feeling something. The result is that we don't feel what we were feeling just a moment ago—at least not with the same intensity.

Think of it like this. Imagine that there are different tiles on the floor. Some tiles send an electric shock through your body when you stand on them. But the shocks stop if you move to another spot on the floor. Similarly, moving from feeling to watching your feelings makes a difference.

The effect may be small, but it is undoubtedly present. And as you get a taste of watching, the feeling of relief can become more and more well-defined and clear to you.

The way to taste the effect of watching is to watch. You will notice that you feel slightly different, maybe less horrible than before. And as you continue to watch, you become more aware of the difference.

I have described this process in detail in another book (*How to Love Obnoxious People and Why*). But for now, I will note that watching brings us into a "spot inside the brain," a "space" of some kind. People who meditate or observe themselves regularly are well aware of this space. This spot is very peaceful or blissful.

Watching gives us access to this spot, this space.

It's almost like being in the middle of a fight versus watching it from a distance. When we are in the grip of a high-intensity emotion, it can feel unpleasant and toxic. But if we move away and watch from another spot, we don't feel the intensity, tension, or unpleasantness.

Here is something from Lucretius. He wasn't talking about the process I am describing here, but see how he describes someone watching something terrible happening.

He writes that it feels better to be on the shore, watching someone else's misfortune in the water. Lucretius notes that this is not because it is good to feel happy watching someone else suffer (this is not schadenfreude). Instead, it is because you feel relief that you aren't the one in that horrible situation. One feels the same relief watching a battle when you are in no danger. But nothing is more joyful than to be high above, strengthened by wise teachings, watching others wander, laboring and struggling to show how smart they are, to get ahead in life, and to acquire wealth and power. Lucretius gives some valuable advice, addressing his readers in a way no self-help author in this day and age would dare to address readers: "Ah! miserable minds of men, blind hearts! In what darkness of life, in what great dangers ye spend this little span of years! . . . To think that ye should not see that nature cries aloud for nothing else but that pain may be kept far sundered from the body, and that, withdrawn from care and fear, she may enjoy in mind the sense of pleasure!"[16]

The points Lucretius makes are as follows:

1. We spend our lives in "darkness" and "dangers."

2. That what "nature" really wants is for pain to be kept far from us.

3. That "withdrawn" or separated from "care and fear," we may experience pleasure in our minds.

---

16   Bailey, Cyril (translator), 1929. Lucretius On the Nature of Things. Clarendon P.

Granted, Lucretius was, a bit morbidly, talking about watching people drown or kill each other, but the process is analogous to what happens when we watch.

Paraphrasing and applying Lucretius's words to the watching situation, we can draw the following parallel:

1. We spend our lives swept up in this or that emotion, thought, feeling, or nanny mental state.

2. We have the option of not being swept up in this way.

3. We can separate or distance ourselves from the troubling feelings and thoughts and feel much better.

THE NEXT STEPS

After we watch, we detach ourselves momentarily from the feeling, emotion, or thought. Like Lucretius watching a poor fellow suffer, we watch ourselves from a short distance, a very short mental distance. The relief may not seem like much initially, but it will grow as we get more used to this practice.

Once we have the distance, we also understand another thing: the *I* that is watching is not the same as the *I* that is suffering through emotion or feeling. The watching *I* can, therefore, easily say *meh* to the *I* with the problem.

This is the equivalent of holding something at arm's length while you examine and evaluate it. The point is not to believe thoughts or feelings popping into your head. So, we say *meh* to emphasize that we are not falling for it. A feeling of envy, anger, etc., may *pretend* that it is important, urgent, or correct, but we know better. We hold these at a tiny mental distance, not an arm's length, but this distance is enough to get the job done.

We follow this by questioning the assumptions behind that feeling, emotion, opinion, or nanny mental state. Then, we say *meh* to those assumptions as well. That's like saying,

"Assumptions, you've had your say, but I am not impressed. I don't immediately believe you. I will put you to the test. I will examine you. I will evaluate the evidence."

The watching *I* now holds the assumptions at the same tiny mental distance. It doesn't immediately buy into them.

After the evidence is in, it usually discards or discounts the assumptions.

Then what?

Moving away from the negative, watching, and meh-ing creates room. Mental room.

Now that we have the room and space, we can usher in the positive.

This positive is what I call the good stuff.

These are valuable skills. The interesting or strange thing is that these skills have been drummed into our heads since we were babies. They are not secrets or big mysteries. But most of the time, we don't seem to benefit from them.

We all know what they are. Maybe, because they are so obvious and well-known, we don't pay the attention that we ought to pay to these skills.

Another problem is that many people think they know these skills or what they mean. I assure you that these skills have an inner dynamic that can revolutionize our lives.

By inner dynamic, I mean that these skills or techniques can help us use our minds and bodies in a better way.

SKILL 1: HUMILITY

We are not talking about fake humility. Fake humility is essentially a form of pride. It manifests in several different ways.

One way is to think that you are more humble than others. "Nobody is as humble as I am!" is not, of course, humility. The reason is that anyone who says this is proud of being humble. And therefore, he is proud. Humility, in this case, is like a mask or outer covering that the person is wearing. As we will see, humility is all about not wearing a mask or covering.

Ridiculous charades occur when two or several such "humble" people are together. They may try to outdo each other in their humility. This is competitiveness, pure and simple. The individuals may appear outwardly humble, but the inner dynamic of humility is absent.

It is almost as if, instead of eating apples, someone balanced several apples carefully on top of their body, carrying them around like badges. Such a person may appear to be "full of apples" (analogous to "full of humility"), but effectively, the nutrition in those apples has not been absorbed. These apples are merely decorative.

Similarly, this kind of humility may make people feel good about themselves, but it lacks the inner dynamic that genuine humility provides.

Decorative humility is not humility.

The other variety of pseudohumility could be called "thinking yourself humble." This is how it works. You hear that humility is good for you. So, you think in ways that appear humble to you. You don't drive the fanciest car; you wear shabby clothes and may go out of your way to be meek and submissive. Again, it is like carrying an apple on your head instead of eating it. Humility must be eaten and absorbed for it to provide what it can.

The third variety has shades of the other two. You are humble because you want to be seen as humble, although not to the pathological degree when competing to be the most humble. In this variety, you again pick the outward features of what you think humility should be and then "wear this humility" so that others (and you) can see you being humble. The apple remains on the outside. It may give comfort that you have the humility apple, and others may point to you as an example of humility, but you aren't benefiting from the humility like you could.

I want to emphasize that the people involved in the humility charades may not be doing so for selfish reasons. In other words, for most of us, humility has been presented by society and culture to be thinking, feeling, and behaving in a certain way. Mistakenly, we have assumed that we will be humble if we think or do things in a certain way.

Of course, at a social level, it is nice to have people who are not constantly bragging and tooting their horns or being so wrapped up in pride that they make life difficult for themselves and others. However, there are other benefits as well, and these can be obtained if one approaches humility with a different attitude.

It begins with considering the nanny mental state, any nanny mental state, but especially a state that is troubling, anxiety-provoking, irritating, and frustrating. Or any nanny mental state causing difficulties because of a *fixed, inflexible way of thinking*.

Such nanny mental states have an *I* convinced that it has to be "its way or the highway." This *I* imagines that its thoughts are absolutely, unquestionably correct. Every other way of thinking (from its point of view) is wrong.

The attitude of humility says meh to this absolutist thinking. It says, "It seems so, but maybe I am wrong. Let me investigate with a clear mind."

That's all there is to it. To be truly humble is not to be outwardly humble but to approach life and your attitude to different things with humility, which means openness. Openness to information—information that may prove you wrong.

It is the opposite of the attitude of prejudgment. When we buy into and believe our nanny mental states, we have prejudged. We have accepted that our nanny mental states are telling us the whole truth and nothing but the truth.

In this book, we have been meh-ing our opinions/feelings/emotions and then meh-ing our assumptions. We have said to ourselves, "I don't believe this state of pride, envy, or anger or feeling bummed about the way life is going. The state(s) seem compelling on the face of it, but I don't want to be fooled by an incorrect understanding of things."

We go back and forth within ourselves, trying to get as close as possible to a correct way of thinking.

And we can do so because we haven't doggedly accepted whatever nanny mental state pops up inside our minds.

This is humility. *Humility is being able to view nanny mental states in an objective or nearly-objective way. We put ourselves in a holding pattern with our mehs. We examine, we evaluate, and we consider the facts. If the state appears to be mistaken, we discard it and move on. That is to say, meh-ve on.*

What about outward humility with a nonshowy lifestyle? Isn't that humility?

It could be. If you, in the after-meh phase, reject your love affair with yourself and discard pride, envy, status symbols, and the things in life that are only for show, then I imagine you would appear humble to others. But this humility is not a mask. This appearance is the result of an inner attitude, an inner dynamic.

When you wear a mask of humility, what have you done? You have imposed a state upon yourself, a nanny mental state that declares, "'I' am humble because I am outwardly humble." Of course, as you can readily appreciate, imposing or putting on any mask or putting on a nanny mental state is the opposite of true humility. True humility questions nanny mental states and puts them aside. Those pointless or useless states fall away when their pointlessness and uselessness are understood.

It is like imagining that scattering cereal outside your house can keep hippopotamuses away. You can do this, but if you live in most places where there aren't any hippopotamuses, the method will obviously seem to work. You could get into a fight with your neighbor who complains about the messy mountains of cereal outside your house on the road. In this situation, consider how humility may be helpful. Applying humility to the nanny mental state that believes in anti-hippo-cereal-scattering, you might begin by saying to yourself that not everything you believe or think is correct and that it is possible for you to be wrong. You could then question your belief in the efficacy of cereal scattering. When you do so, you may understand and accept that there aren't any hippos around unless you're in a zoo (and not even in all zoos). And so you may then ask yourself what the point of unnecessarily scattering cereal is to keep the nonexistent hippos away. This would hopefully cause you to stop behaving in this way.

Humility allows us to free ourselves of unnecessary or debilitating nanny mental states.

SKILL 2: PATIENCE

Imagine a fly buzzing around you. It is only a fly, so you disregard it. But it bothers you, so you must keep swishing it away.

You don't think much of the fly. The fly can harm you because who knows where it has been? Flies are well-known to be attracted to filthy things, like poop. Then, they might land on a cake, rubbing their legs together and transferring the poop-ish bacteria on the cake. But, in the grand scheme of things, we can protect ourselves from a fly with adequate precautions. They are only flies, for crying out loud.

Swishing away a fly is the equivalent of meh. You might be bored. No problem. It's a fly. You can quickly swish it with meh.

But feelings, emotions, thoughts, opinions, fears, worries—these can keep surfacing and resurfacing. And so you may have to keep swishing them away.

In practical terms, it means meh-ing them repeatedly.

We don't let these mental troubles trouble us because we can see through them. Because of humility, we don't think we know everything. We investigate the troubles with an open mind and find that they aren't so troubling.

But then the trouble reemerges, maybe not as vigorously as before. What do we do?

We meh again. And again. Feeling X. Meh. Feeling X again. Meh. Feeling X again. Meh. Feeling X again. Meh, and so on.

We know that we don't remain in our nanny mental states forever. Few people would say something like "I was jealous thirty years ago and have been continuously jealous since that time." Even if you feel perpetually jealous, you will still experience other states. Our states keep flickering like dying fluorescent lamps. They fluctuate in intensity or get replaced by other states. Our states vary depending on the circumstances.

This ability to keep meh-ing and swishing away the fly is patience.

We don't get the desired result right away, or we get it for a short while, and then the result fades away. Does this mean we give up? No. It means we keep at it. We keep doing what we need to do until we can do something else.

That is patience.

If you've ever boiled water, you know it takes a certain amount of time to boil. If it takes five minutes for the water to boil, you are unlikely to give up on the boiling project because "It's been *three whole* minutes, and it's still not boiling. Enough already!"

But when it comes to affairs of the mind, we may not be so understanding. We want results right away. Also, we may desire dramatic results. It's as if you are expecting an instant, delicious cupcake to emerge when you've just started preheating the oven. I know no one will do this, but we may expect too much from our mental machinery.

When we watch, we experience relief, but it may not seem like much in the beginning. However, it is enough. The feeling deepens or becomes more noticeable as we become more adept at watching.

This, too, is patience. We patiently apply the technique, and we will get some results. Maybe not as impressive as we would like. Here is what I mean.

When we watch, we no longer feel the intensity of emotion we were feeling only a moment ago. This feeling is very short-lived. You are feeling the absence of something, which can feel like nothing.

Nothing doesn't seem impressive. But this nothing can bring relief.

We may be feeling dissatisfaction. We go through the drill. We watch, we meh, we meh the assumptions, we understand how dissatisfaction works. Dissatisfaction disappears for a bit. We may feel neutral, nothing, and be "blank" for a short while. This "blank" state is a "nothing" state in which we feel nothing. It might not even register, even though it is the absence of an irritating, annoying state.

Then dissatisfaction might return, perhaps a bit differently, maybe in a muted form.

We do the same thing again.

Patience is doing what works over and over again.

The idea is not to make incorrect decisions or take wrong actions because an out-of-touch, dissatisfied nanny mental state commands the *I* to do so. We watch, we meh, we meh-ve on, and we patiently keep doing this—because it works.

Imagine a tourist visiting the Grand Canyon. She is fascinated by the marvel of the Colorado River cutting through the rocks, making the Canyon take its shape. The tourist asks the river at the bottom of the Canyon, "This place is amazing. How long did it take you to make this canyon?" Amazingly, the river can talk. So it answers, "Oh, only a few million years." That is what I mean by patience. Keep doing what works, and we will notice the benefits and move on to more productive ways of being. (Incidentally, the consensus is that the Grand Canyon may have taken 5–6 million years to form. Some parts may be much, much older, though.)

Another dimension to patience is combining it with humility to keep investigating and evaluating the evidence.

We are working on a project. Let's call it Project Us. (I don't want to call it Project Me, as that sounds a teensy bit self-centered—even though it is partly accurate since the complete truth about Project Us is that it is about helping everyone, including ourselves.)

In Project Us, we are trying to live with ourselves and others and do the best possible job. "Best possible job" can mean different things to different people. It means we live peacefully and kindly with each other, not hurting each other, and reach our potential if we can. (I will not say we should try to reach our full potential. Of course, we can never realize our full potential. We can only do what we can at any given time, so why get all worked up about not reaching the heights possible for us?)

Project Us requires us to use two skills, at a minimum:

1. Have humility. We acknowledge how little we know and keep ourselves open to helpful information. This will help us make more informed decisions.

2. Have patience to collect information, think about it, and try to understand. And do all this without feeling rushed or getting our "panties in a wad," as one of the main characters in *The Blind Side* says. In this film, Sandra Bullock plays Leigh Anne Tuohy, who adopted Michael Oher, the future football player. She has just dropped both her biological and adopted sons at school. She is watching them walk inside the school. The person behind

her honks, and Sandra Bullock mutters, "Don't get your panties in a wad."

They have a similar saying in England: *Don't get your knickers in a twist.* Many of us tend to tie our psyches (and maybe even our muscles) in knots over big and small things, much like these underwear-related sayings warn us about not getting our underwear twisted or wadded up—which sounds uncomfortable.

Patience is also needed while we wait for situations to resolve. Or if they don't, we try our luck again. Or we try something else. Sometimes, we may just have to wait.

Watching and meh create patience. We separate ourselves from impatient, seemingly urgent thoughts. When we meh, we don't give them much importance. And the urgency dries up. Impatience morphs into patience, giving us time to let the matter incubate and collect useful information.

SKILL 3: GRATITUDE

The joy of being human frequently takes a back seat to other things.

Ordinarily, we revolve around an axis of troubles, pain, miseries, and frustrations.

I remember a fragment of an anecdote. Someone reported seeing first the CEO and then a janitor at an organization. The CEO had a frown, but the janitor had a smile and was singing as he worked. Who was the happier one? Who would you rather be? Speaking for myself, I would prefer to be the CEO. And I think many others would also pick the CEO. Am I right?

If I am right, this suggests that we pick our troubles as much as our troubles pick us.

Remember Lucretius? He said that nothing is more joyful

than to be high above, strengthened by wise teachings, watching others wander, laboring and struggling to show how smart they are, to get ahead in life, and to acquire wealth and power.

Given a choice, most of us would pick wealth and power, even if it meant wandering, laboring, and struggling. Maybe this is why the CEO in the anecdote was less cheerful than the janitor. Perhaps the janitor would meet with Lucretius's approval. Lucretius was an Epicurean who believed in living a life of sensible pleasure. Remember how Lucretius referred to those of us who are running around trying to fulfill our ambitions?

Regardless, here is how I imagine some of us may think about this: *Withdrawn from care and fear . . . pain kept far from the body . . . enjoy the sense of pleasure . . . yes, but if I could be a CEO, surely that would still be better, wouldn't it?*

We have worked through various states that lead to this constant striving that causes the "miserable minds" to spend time in "darkness." Greed, envy, pride, dissatisfaction with our lot in life, boredom—all these motivate us to go after more, more, and yet more.

The antidote to these states is a far more enjoyable one. It is a state of gratitude.

Gratitude is a state that many great religious, spiritual, and philosophical teachers say is available to us all the time.

Is this true? Let's see.

We start with a nanny mental state, in which *I* am not happy with what I have and want to get this or that to find fulfillment.

We watch this nanny mental state, and when we do so, we shift to another *I*—the watching *I*. We meh the nanny mental state, and we meh the faulty assumptions on which the nanny mental state rests. We end up in a mental "space" where we have access to other skills.

One of these is gratitude. Gratitude for what we have, however little.

We may have very few amenities. But, by comparison, many have fewer amenities or none. And so, we can be grateful for what we have.

Or we may be at the absolute bottom regarding resources. We may be among the many millions with almost nothing except health. Well, health is an irreplaceable, fantastic asset. We only realize the value of health when we have lost it.

Or what if we don't even have health? Then what?

Some people have terrible diseases, life-threatening or debilitating illnesses that rob them of every pleasure. How is one supposed to be grateful amid that?

I hope I never have to answer this question. I hope that no one has to answer this question. But the reality is that at least some people may have to answer this question one day.

The fact is that, even though it is constantly surprising to me, some people with awful diseases somehow find gratitude. They do this by focusing on the good, no matter what it is.

And so, although it seems unbelievable to me, some people can achieve this feat. And they do this by accentuating the positive.

In terms of nanny mental states, the complaining, dissatisfied *I* is just one out of many states available to us. But if, amid an unsatisfying, difficult situation, we turn our attention to something nice—anything, really—then a different nanny mental state takes over. This different nanny mental state has a happier, more satisfied *I*.

I don't want to oversimplify, but it is like having a choice to look at something bad or something good. Gratitude is the equivalent of looking at something good, however little, and falling into a nanny mental state that is more pleasing.

Suppose you could look at a plate of revolting, rotting flesh or turn your head and look at a plate with delicious pastries, or chocolate, or even a slice of bread. Or it could be a tiny portion of a slice of bread. Or perhaps only a few particles of bread.

I suppose it is theoretically possible to have nothing to feel grateful for. But for most other people, there might still be something, however small. It is that small something that we can focus on.

Arthur Schopenhauer was a famous pessimistic philosopher who said, "Human life must be some kind of mistake" and that if we had any sympathy for our future generation, we would "spare it the burden of existence" (by not reproducing). Undoubtedly, he was not the most cheerful soul in the world. But he had some rather insightful things to say about gratitude, which is surprising given his dark views. His thoughts on gratitude go along with what we have discussed: "We rarely think of what we have but always of what we lack. Therefore, rather than grateful, we are bitter."

And "whether we are in a pleasant or a painful state depends upon the kind of matter that pervades and engrosses our consciousness and what we compare it to—better and we are envious and sad, worse and we feel grateful and happy." In simpler terms, our nanny mental state can be happy or sad, depending on what we focus on. We can envy those who have more than we do or be grateful that we have more than others.

Given a choice, wouldn't you want to feel better, not worse? Well, gratitude is one way of doing so.

And let's not forget that gratitude has been shown to improve both physical and psychological health. It makes us less aggressive, helps us sleep better, makes us feel less stressed, and enables us to be more resilient. Veterans with more gratitude suffer less from post-traumatic stress disorder. Gratitude may also lower the risk of heart disease.

It has been shown that people who keep a gratitude journal and note a few things they are grateful for daily feel much better about life and are happier. The way to keep a gratitude journal is incredibly easy. You don't even need a journal. A small piece of paper or the back of an envelope would work just fine. All you need to do is write a few things you are grateful for daily.

How many entries you make is entirely up to you. Do you have only one thing for which you are grateful? No problem. Write that thing down. Write it down once, twice, or a few times. Write the same things every day. It doesn't matter. The idea is to concentrate briefly on what you are grateful for and write it down. It doesn't take much time, but the payoff is great.

Gratitude also works great in combination with the other two skills.

Suppose I think, *My life sucks today*.

Immediately, I can meh this and all its assumptions.

I think of all the things I am grateful for.

Feeling better, I investigate, with humility, my life and why it "sucks" today.

The answers are not immediately forthcoming, so I am patient.

Gradually or suddenly, I have an insight or a better understanding of my situation.

Maybe I even realize that my life is not that sucky after all—perhaps it is only a tiny bit sucky. That's still progress.

USEFUL SKILL 4a: FORGIVENESS

Consider what happens when we don't forgive.

Someone does something awful or unforgivable to us. We can't let go.

Our nanny mental state is one in which *I* fixates on the wrong someone did to us. Unsurprisingly, we feel angry and frustrated. We resent the person who wronged us. We want revenge.

Our insides get consumed with bitter feelings.

Please understand that I am not saying that people who harm others should not receive justice. I only want to point out that there is no point in having harmful, negative emotions accumulate inside us. Justice is one thing. Harming ourselves with toxic thoughts is another. Most people would agree that while justice makes sense, hurting ourselves is pointless.

The advantage of forgiveness is as follows: In one fell swoop, we eliminate the troubles inside our heads.

The nanny mental state, the *I* spawns a noxious brew of unpleasant thoughts: thoughts of getting even, of striking mental or physical blows, of hurting those who have caused it hurt. This is the state before one forgives.

And if we forgive, what happens then?

Instantly, we have a different nanny mental state. One in which there is an absence of these disturbing thoughts. Minus these thoughts, we feel instantly better.

So, how do we get to this state? How do we forgive?

STEP 1: Watch the feeling of being unable to forgive when it arises. How does it feel inside the head and the body? What sensations does it produce? Simply watch and take note of whatever you think and feel.

STEP 2: You say *meh* to the feeling (either loudly or mentally, depending on whether you are alone or in company).

STEP 3: Next, you ask, "Why am I unable to forgive?"

STEP 4: You answer, "Because what this person did was unforgivable. If I forgive, he will get away with it. Some things can't be forgiven. I can't help these feelings. I deserve to strike back."

STEP 5: You say *meh* to these assumptions. Assumptions are not inherently correct; they must be proven.

STEP 6: After-meh: Play with the assumptions and think more accurately about them.

The assumptions make an incorrect connection between

justice and not forgiving. But, as I mentioned earlier, there is no connection. Justice is not only desirable, but it is also necessary (otherwise, people will continue to wrong others, which is not correct). But what does justice have to do with not forgiving? Why must we feel bad inside and hurt ourselves internally with negative emotions?

Isn't correctly/legally administered justice about punishing those who have committed wrongs or crimes against others? Isn't justice the mechanism for payback for a wrong done by someone? So, when justice is delivered, don't you think that the payback—punishment—balances, however inadequately or poorly, the wrong that has been done? We live in a world where perfect punishment may be impossible, and going after it is a recipe for frustration and disappointment.

Understand me. Some crimes and wrongs are so dreadful that there can't be any punishment to fit the crime. When someone murders millions, simply killing that person can't possibly equal the crime. But how much more can one punish? Torture? Is any amount of torture equal to the enormity of some crimes? And remember, when you torture, if you torture, you are doing so from a groundswell of hatred and hostility, both harmful to you. So why torture? Our society has punishments in place for crimes, which have been agreed upon as appropriate. Why not stick to the norms of our society when it comes to delivering justice?

When society punishes and delivers justice, it is a form or part of forgiveness. How? Well, there are two possibilities.

First, the punishment may genuinely balance out the crime. If it does, that's great, and we can assume that the punished person has had their slate cleaned for that particular crime. We can move on. When we move on and stop blaming this individual for what he or she did, isn't that forgiveness? It is forgiveness arrived at by way of justice.

"No, not possible," some would say. I would recommend

that these people say *meh* to their thoughts. Not forgiving, not moving on, will cause tremendous dissatisfaction.

And remember, not every wrongdoer or crime will receive justice. Sadly, many wrongs probably go unpunished. So, if we cannot forgive, we will remain in anger, irritation, resentment, hostility, and unhappiness.

The second possibility concerns the things that can't be forgiven. Yes, I agree with you. Some things can't be forgiven. It may seem impossible to forgive certain things. I find it difficult to forgive the actions of certain people (especially mass murderers and cruel people). But we can try to reason about this. If you don't forgive, you only hurt yourself. How does that make sense? I hope that most of us, when we see—really *see*—that we are doing something useless or harmful, will stop.

This leads to the next assumption: People can argue (like I argue) that *I can't help feeling like this*. Yes, that is true in a sense. It is only true from the point of view of the nanny mental state, in which the *I* can't help feeling like this. But we have *other* nanny mental states, other *I*'s that are possible. These states are close to us. We only have to reach out to them.

The way of reaching out to them is simple:

1. You watch.

2. You ignore the importance of the nanny mental state (this is saying *meh*).

3. You realize the pointlessness of the nanny mental state (this is saying *meh* to the inaccurate or incomplete assumptions).

4. You move on to a different nanny mental state, where a slightly different, more realistic *I* takes hold of you. This *I* can be a grateful *I*, a loving *I*, a kind *I*. Yes, says this *I*, a terrible wrong has been committed. But *I*, for my sanity,

equilibrium, and peace of mind, will focus on the good things in life. If this evil person gets justice, that would be great. But if not, *I* will not injure myself in the process.

And this is how one can reach forgiveness. But we are not done yet. We need something else: *forget-ness*.

USEFUL SKILL 4b: FORGET-NESS

In a way, forget-ness is an essential meh technique, or you could say it is the "most meh" skill of all. Forget-ness plays a role in every meh. We will see how at the end of this chapter.

Some people say, "I've forgiven, but I've not forgotten."

Is it possible to forgive and not forget? Can forgiveness without forgetting be called forgiveness?

I think it depends on the forgetting.

If you hold a grudge, some level of wariness, or low-level resentment, you have not completely expunged troubles from your mind. Some negativity remains inside you.

From a mental standpoint, the critical move is to steer clear of troubling thoughts from your mind. So, if you still retain some baseline irritation, a little seed of annoyance, you have not become completely clear. Or, to put it differently, you are in a nanny mental state that is not negativity-free.

But you can't forget completely either. If X has wronged you, you must remember to avoid this person or protect yourself from getting wronged again.

The need is to *forget without forgetting*. It is a very special kind of forgetting. In it, you remember that you don't want to get harmed in the future by X, but at the same time, you "forget." I am using the word "forget" in a very specific way. We must "forget" the nanny mental state that holds the negative emotion.

I will repeat: We must "forget" the nanny mental state that holds the negative emotion.

But we can still have a nanny mental state in which the *I* is aware that it has to be careful. *But without the negativity.*

Forget-ness is the word I use to refer to a state in which we have "forgotten" the state that retains the negative, the troubles. The state minus the troubles equals forget-ness. Here are the steps:

1. You watch.
2. You ignore the importance of the nanny mental state that hasn't "forgotten" (this is saying *meh*).
3. You realize the pointlessness of the nanny mental state (this is saying *meh* to the inaccurate assumptions).
4. You move on to a different nanny mental state, one in which a different nanny mental state takes over, the kind described above. The nanny mental state with negativity is "forgotten."

This kind of "forgetting" might seem fake to you. But it is not. It is real.

Think of a time when you were hungry recently. At that time, you were in a nanny mental state that was experiencing hunger. Are you still in that nanny mental state? Obviously not. So, have you "forgotten" that state? Of course, you have, in the sense that it is no longer there. In the same way, a nanny mental state that is no longer present, no matter how real it was a few moments ago, is "forgotten."

This is what I mean by "forget-ness."

Now I will share why I think that forget-ness is an essential meh skill:

When we forgive and then forget, we "forget" the unhelpful nanny mental state. That is the goal of every meh, so "forget-ness" is key to all the mehs we have discussed. In every situation, we have said *meh* to a particular nanny mental state—and therefore, we have "forgotten" that particular nanny mental state.

But now comes a question: Exactly how does one forget? It's not like you can order yourself, "I command you to forget X." The command contains X. And so, the very order makes you remember X, which is not forgotten.

The way to forget-ness cannot be through a command, through force. It has to happen "naturally." Naturally means "the way things happen in the mind," with a little help. The emphasis is on the "little." But a little help goes a long way.

Suppose you wish to forget nanny mental state X. How do you do it?

It is straightforward, and we have been doing this throughout this book.

Nanny mental states are like adulterous spouses with roving eyes. Or I should say, we are a bit like unfaithful lovers. We love and inhabit one nanny mental state, and then, moments later, we find ourselves in another. This happens on its own thousands of times each day.

What we are attempting is a bit more conscious, targeted mental "adultery."

When we meh our nanny mental state and their assumptions, and when we think about more positive attitudes and states, we are helping nature along. It's like placing enticing lovers before our roving eyes. (Please note, I don't support actual adultery! This is only an analogy.) For example, we might be in an envious nanny mental state, but once we understand things differently, we now have another fresh, inviting, more positive nanny mental state. What's a mental Romeo like us to do? We fall headlong into the positive nanny mental state. The old nanny mental state is ditched.

Presto, we have forgotten! Forget-ness is a lot like falling in love—without the love. We move—or meh-ve—from the negative nanny mental state into the positive one because our minds appreciate the value of doing so.

In the case of toxic states like envy, being dissatisfied, or feeling vengeful and frustrated, forget-ness brings great relief. The removal of the negative state feels good, even if it is for a moment. It creates a taste for more. With practice, we start staying increasingly in positive nanny mental states.

Nudists will no doubt disagree with me, but clothes make life much less complicated in a particular way. I bring this up only because it relates to a point I have been trying to make about forget-ness and meh.

All of us have private parts. If we didn't wear clothes, these parts would be out there, in the open, a distraction for those who don't want to be assailed by private parts all around them. Clothes are a nice compromise. The private parts are still there, but we are no longer distracted by them.

Forget-ness is almost like this. We have all kinds of nanny mental states. But when we shift our attention, the old, problematic nanny mental states disappear from view. As they have been "clothed."

USEFUL SKILL 5a: GENEROSITY

Pride. Envy. Self-esteem. Dissatisfaction. The feeling that life is unfair. Boredom. Anger. Worry. Greed. Perfectionism. Stress. These are the issues we have discussed in this book. If you look at most of the stuff that bothers us, a common theme emerges: *Mental troubles afflict us when we are concerned with ourselves.*

Pride—*I* am the best, excellent, superb, etc.

Envy—*I* must get what the other person has.

Self-esteem—*I* don't feel good about myself (low self-esteem); *I* am the best there is; *I* am the greatest thing since sliced bread (excessive self-esteem).

Dissatisfaction—*I* don't like the way things are going in my life.

The feeling that life is unfair—*I* am not getting what *I* think *I* should get; if only life were fair.

Boredom—*I* don't have enough excitement or enjoyment or something to engage me.

Anger—*I* am mad because things haven't gone my way.

Worry—*I* am concerned that things might not go my way.

Greed—*I* want more.

Perfectionism—*I* want to be perfect and do everything perfectly.

Stress—*I* have too much on my plate, more than *I* can handle.

Do you see it? It's all *I*, *I*, *I*. *I* this and *I* that.

We don't have a global, all-encompassing *I*. It's not as if this *I* is *all* of you or me.

No.

It is a tiny, mental, neurochemical blip inside our brains. The *I* that is the product of a nanny mental state.

Hopefully, we have learned what to do with these pesky nanny mental states by now. We meh them, ignore them, and meh-ve on to better states.

This is where generosity comes in.

Generosity is the *uber*-meh, the ultimate meh. It is a poke in the eye of troubling nanny mental states.

You can think of it like this: Suppose I am worried about X. This is equivalent to saying, "I have a nanny mental state that is giving me the impression that *I* have something to worry about." Let us suppose, for this illustration, that this is a "what-if" worry, a worry you can't do anything about.

Now, here comes generosity to metaphorically stick its thumb up this nanny mental state's nose. Generosity means giving away something to someone in need. It has two parts: "giving away" and "someone in need."

You could "give away" some help or money or spend some time fixing someone else's problem. But you are "giving away" a lot more than that.

You are "giving away" your nanny mental state. By concentrating on "giving away" something of value to someone else, you have ditched a nanny mental state that was bothering you!

And where is that worried nanny mental state? It has been "forgotten."

I don't mean to imply that we should be generous only because we want to help ourselves. That would defeat the purpose.

No. The correct approach is to be generous and "give away." You will help someone, and you will help yourself, but the intention is not to do this selfishly.

When you are able, even amid all this stress, if you have but a moment to spare, give your attention to someone else's problem.

You will know what I mean if you deal with children or needy or whiny people. Sometimes, it feels like everyone wants their problems solved when I am up to my ears in demanding issues. Stressed out. Unable to take on more, thinking, *How much more can I do?*

And yet, there is a marvelous paper by Cassie Mogilner, Zoë Chance, and Michael I. Norton titled "Giving Time Gives You Time." What an intriguing title! It encapsulates, completely and pithily, what Dr. Mogilner and her colleagues found: *that if you don't have enough time, you can give some of it away, and doing so can give you time.* Let me explain.

If you think you don't have enough time (hello, stress), you can give some of it away. Doing so increases your feeling of "self-efficacy." It gives a feeling that "I can do more" or "I am more able." This also stretches (pun intended) your sense of being able to do more with the time you have. In other words, your subjective sense of "time affluence" increases. Time affluence is the idea that you have enough or more than enough time to get your work done.

Note that you still have the same amount of time you had before. But your feeling of being able to do more in the same amount of time has increased. This belief gives you the motivation and courage to do more without getting bogged down by self-doubts that you might fail. Can you still fail? Sure. But you can act with the belief that you won't, and you can get the job done. And who knows, you might do so without failing. The end result? The job gets done.

You could say that your nanny mental state with an *I* that felt time-poor is transformed into one with an *I* that feels time-rich. This subjective feeling makes you feel better, and you will probably be able to achieve more (maybe only a bit more) with reduced stress.

What an idea!

It is like the old saying that if you want something done, you should ask a busy person to do it. Maybe some busy people are busy doing stuff because they feel they have lots of time and can move efficiently through many tasks.

Giving time away is a form of generosity, so the next time you feel overwhelmed, seriously think about being a little generous with your time (if you can; if you can't, at least don't snap at someone who asks you for help!). You might feel much better about the time you have left to take care of your stuff.

We can see that generosity, by saying *meh* to an unproductive nanny mental state and being unimpressed by a seemingly oppressive nanny mental state, gives you freedom. Or it may only be a *sense* of freedom (a sense that can help you feel better and, strangely enough, help you do more, even when you—or a boneheaded *I*—thought you couldn't possibly do more).

USEFUL SKILL 5b: NOT TOO MUCH SELF-INTEREST

Not having too much self-interest is an essential skill and fits right in with the whole philosophy of the power of meh.

Self-interest is a nanny mental state in which the *I* is concerned for its well-being and prosperity. We have to look after ourselves. We can't be oblivious and enter situations that could harm us. We have to do our due diligence and protect ourselves. But there is a sense in which we can go overboard.

Most of the mental troubles we have discussed (and others that we haven't) are rooted in an excessive preoccupation with ourselves.

That is to say, we are preoccupied with an *I* associated with a particular nanny mental state. This *I* wants to look after itself. If we remove the *I* in the examples we've looked at previously—with envy, pride, etc.—no mental problem is left.

But how does one get to such a no-*I* state?

Very simple. We meh. That is to say, we engage in forget-ness.

We take the nanny mental state we're in. We realize that this nanny mental state has an *I* interested in propagating and perpetuating its values and opinions. These opinions are the problem. So we can simply say *meh*. We are not impressed or moved by this *I*. We say *meh* to its assumptions. And then, because we realize that we are better off without this *I*, we simply focus on something else. This *something else* is a more positive, helpful thing or attitude. This is what we have been doing all along.

The key is to slip into forget-ness and forget the *I*. Freed from the desire to feed the needs of *I*, we feel relieved and can devote interest to something that might be helpful to ourselves and others.

Consider what happened to poor William Henry Harrison. He was the ninth president of the United States, but his tenure lasted only thirty-two days. Some say his death was from pneumonia (others disagree) and could have been an example of death by inauguration speech. Let me explain.

At his inauguration on March 4, 1841, President Harrison, probably carried away by the joy of his success, gave an 8,445-word inauguration speech, which lasted about 1 hour and 45 minutes. He did so in a damp setting, with temperatures probably in the forties (Fahrenheit), without a hat, a coat, or gloves. He is reported to have insisted on giving this speech in the bitter cold without adequate cover. Many people believe, perhaps incorrectly, that the extreme length in the cold may have caused him to succumb to pneumonia on April 4, 1841. He was sixty-eight.

Maybe this story is untrue. Some people say he died of typhoid. But even if it is not true, it has a teaching point. His *I* insisted on a particular course of action. His *I-interest* may have been fatal.

I-interest can cause difficulties. Influenced by our *I-interest*, we can do all sorts of things, burden ourselves with too many ambitions, and take on unnecessary headaches.

And a way to jump out of *I-interest* is through forget-ness of *I*—through meh.

USEFUL SKILL 6: KINDNESS TO OTHERS

Kindness is in the same neighborhood as generosity.

There is nothing revolutionary or counterintuitive about being kind. All major religions and philosophies recommend kindness. Scientific studies show that being compassionate is linked to better health, more happiness, less worry, fewer negative emotions, less distress, reduced IL-6 (the molecule associated with diabetes, Alzheimer's, lupus erythematosus, rheumatoid arthritis, and atherosclerosis), more able to receive help from others, less likely to be bullied, reduced blood pressure, a feeling of greater social connection, and inspiration to others to be compassionate.

The question arises: How is one to be compassionate? The answer is that it is pretty easy and goes right to the heart of meh.

Recall that when you feel annoyed, frustrated, or peeved for any reason, you are in the grip of a nanny mental state that makes your *I* feel that way.

If you say *meh* to that feeling (and meh to any assumptions you can identify), then you can think kindly of someone or something with a very simple mental maneuver.

This may seem like you're faking it, and you're right. *You're faking it.* But it doesn't matter, and believe me when I tell you that it can lead to a real feeling—a feeling that you truly feel and is not made up in this fake way. Here's an example.

Recently, I had the distinct displeasure of dealing with someone who behaved terribly.

I wanted to respond with revenge. However, I understood that forgiveness and forget-ness were better approaches. So I applied them.

Immediately, I felt relief. Relief from the burden of having to strike back. Relief from having to do something drastic (and unnecessary).

Now, with more freedom, I was able to think kindly. How? I wished this person well—the one who had misbehaved. That's it. Initially, it felt a bit fake, but the taste of kindness is sweet. And once you start tasting it, you carry on with real kindness (or something close to it).

You can choose to think kindly almost any time you want.
You start with a negative nanny mental state.
You meh this state.
You fake kindness, think kindly, and wish people well.
You do this by saying or thinking something like "I wish for X to do well, feel better, be happy, and be free from troubles. I

wish these good things for all people—friend or foe." If you'd rather not include foes, by all means, include only friends and people you don't have any negative feelings for.

When you do this, you enter a nanny mental state with positive feelings.

And this nanny mental state feels much better.

Even if it is fake, it is still sweet. With time, you will acquire a taste for it and be able to think kindly of others more routinely. You will feel better and happier, and your physical health might improve over the long run.

The other way to generate kindness is to understand why the person behaved like a jerk. There has to be a reason, right? Can you put yourself in their place?

Most people don't set out to be jerks. They behave the way they do because of the way they see things. Also, let's not forget that any of us can misbehave. And I am sure many of us have. It is not as if the jerk is so very different from us. He probably isn't that different. Most of us have the seeds of jerkiness inside us.

This may seem overly simplistic, but I want to mention it. If you eat something bitter, your mouth will acquire a bitter taste. If you eat something sweet, the taste in your mouth will be correspondingly sweet.

Our nanny mental states are like that. We have a choice to think bitterly or sweetly. One of the easiest ways to think "sweetly" is to think kindly.

If you are feeling neutral, without strong negative emotions, then it is not difficult to think kindly of others.

But if you feel upset for some reason or are in the grip of some negativity, work through it by watching and meh-ing. You can think kindly once you have a more realistic understanding of the situation.

Kind thoughts can thus be added after any of the mehs discussed in this book. They fill your mind with pleasantness.

Finally, let us consider actual kindness to others.

By building up the kind thinking muscles, we can now be kind to others.

You won't want to be kind to others if you are annoyed. Why not? You are filled with a bitter nanny mental state.

But if you are annoyed or angry, you can meh the anger and its assumptions, engage in some forget-ness, and then dive into kindness. Be nice to someone, even if it is only to smile. Smiling, it is well-known, can make you feel better because the brain gets confused by the smiling action of facial muscles. Smiling can make the brain think you are happy, even when you aren't. Therefore, technically speaking, when you smile, you are happy, even if it is for an instant. You instantly enter a happier nanny mental state when you smile.

Being kind to others is not rocket science. One can be polite, courteous, and gracious—whatever is possible, whatever the situation allows.

I hope you don't think I am merely advocating kindness as a feel-good drug. It certainly helps us, but if pursued with self-interest, it becomes tainted.

There is a better reason for helping others: The world needs our help. How about helping others because we could all do with a helping hand without expecting something in return? Our motivation shouldn't be to feel great or be congratulated. This avoids the self-interest trap.

USEFUL SKILL 7: KINDNESS TO YOURSELF

Nanny mental states see things in a simple way: their way.

An *I* that many of us have commands us to be a valuable member of society. We are thus driven, to varying degrees, to achieve this or that. The actual achievements will depend on the society or subgroup to which we belong. For example, most of us are not trying to find a revolutionary mathematical theorem—simply because most of us are not mathematicians. But those who inhabit mathematical circles have mathematical ambitions. They want to make a name for themselves—this is what their peer group, their subculture, demands.

Our many mental troubles fixate on ambitions:

Pride—*I* must achieve this because my self-esteem demands it, and *I* am that good.

Greed—*I* must achieve that because if *I* don't, *I* will have a lot less and be insecure.

Envy—*I* must achieve this because others have.

Dissatisfaction—*I* am dissatisfied because I haven't achieved this or that.

The feeling that life is unfair—*I* haven't achieved this, and I think I should.

And so on.

Note that *I* is always hard on itself, pushing us to chase a goal because *I* wants it.

This makes us run after different goals. There is no doubt that we can't possibly get everything we want. Thus, our nanny mental state is not pleased with us when we fail. We are not happy with ourselves. We may blame others, but we may blame ourselves as well.

The solution is to watch and meh this as fast as possible. The assumption behind the pushy *I* is that *I* must have what it wants. But that is nonsense for the following reasons:

I's come and go. To imagine that an *I* is the ultimate truth is incorrect.

I's depend on assumptions that may not be true. We have already seen that greed, envy, pride, dissatisfaction, etc., are based on assumptions that are not entirely correct.

Thus, our job is to be kind to ourselves and nurture ourselves in the after-meh phase. No matter what else we do, we can meh the *I* that is making us go after this or that.

Remember that when we are in the grip of a nanny mental state, the stakes seem high to *I*. The important point is that they *seem high*. The moment we switch from this nanny mental state to a different, more positive one, the stakes don't seem to matter much. This is almost like the quote (with different versions attributed to several people, including Henry Kissinger and Wallace Sayre), "The reason that university politics is so vicious is because stakes are so small." This saying is funny because it is absurd. Vicious fighting for small stakes? It is so ridiculous, right? And yet, while we remain moored to an unproductive *I*, we run after peanuts. In *Learning How to Learn*, Idries Shah quotes Rumi asking his readers when they will stop desiring nuts and raisins.[17]

Once we get past *I* by watching and meh-ing, we can say to ourselves that there are two things in life: There is what we can do—our best. The best is in our control. Given the situation, how energized we feel, and how capable we are, we do whatever we can.

But then there's everything else. The results are not up to us. What others think of us is not up to us. Whether it rains is not up to us. How others behave, drive, or act is not up to us.

Once we've done our best, the rest is not up to us. And as for the best, what I mean by this is that we make a good-faith effort. We clear our minds of negativity, study the problem or the matter before us, and then apply reasonable effort. That's it.

If we understand that we can't control the outcome, we will be relaxed. We won't bash ourselves. To quote Tony Horton, "Do your best, forget the rest."

If you find that you are hard on yourself, you can easily apply self-compassion.

USEFUL SKILL 8: BEING EVEN-TEMPERED

A common feature of nanny mental states is that they suddenly appear, assume center stage, and, after a while, move on.

---

17 Shah, Idries, 2020. *Learning How to Learn*. ISF Publishing. Kindle.

The power of meh is to help them move on faster, especially when they are unproductive.

The key is not to turn into Mr. Spock and be a cold-blooded, emotionless psychopath. No. We laugh when we are happy, cry when we are sad, and participate in life's joys and sadness. But this doesn't mean we are on a constant emotional roller coaster.

We think and feel based on a combination of nature and nurture. Our feelings may seem inevitable, but someone who doesn't have the same mixture of nature and nurture may feel differently.

When we get caught up in nanny mental state X, the whole world is seen through the lens of this state. The nanny mental state changes by watching, meh-ing, and then entering the after-meh stage. We are no longer in the same state as before.

We are in a calmer, more relaxed place. Here, we are open to other possibilities. We see a bigger picture than we saw before. Before, we were shackled to a challenging nanny mental state that was coloring our perception. Now, we are freed up.

We enter a state where we have the potential to discover better solutions to our problems simply because we are not trapped in an emotional firestorm. Thinking clearly requires us to have space. Sometimes, you may need to "get away," go for a walk, stretch your legs, or step away from wherever you are. These maneuvers help you detach yourself from the situation. And when you do so, a solution may come to you.

This is why you may be hot on the heels of a problem, getting a headache—and the solution appears when you stop trying so hard. You may be taking a break when you finally figure something out. You liberated yourself, briefly, from an oppressive nanny mental state. When you did so, the solution offered itself, probably because other parts of your brain became engaged in the process—parts that could see different aspects of the problem and apply their brainpower to it.

The history of science has numerous examples of scientists stumbling on a solution when resting or taking some time off from a problem. But I am sure we have all had our share of smaller, satisfying discoveries when we were not caught up in the drama of the problem.

The after-meh phase comes when we have observed the nanny mental state and (A) meh-ed it and (B) meh-ed the assumptions.

What comes after (A) and (B) is a time of reflection, when possibilities open up before us. The after-meh phase is one in which we are relaxed and even-tempered. We are not running around wildly, angrily, trying to find satisfaction for this or that irritating thing.

Or we can express it like this: After-meh equals an even-tempered state.

Thus, applying the meh process results in our ability to be relatively free of maddening or troubling nanny mental states. The after-meh state is an even-tempered one, and it is, therefore, a critical aspect of the power of meh.

USEFUL SKILL 9: BEING A GOOD FRIEND, THINKING OF YOURSELF AS THE HOST

A simplified way of applying the after-meh skills of kindness, generosity, and an even temperament is to think of it this way: Imagine you are the host of the world around you.

Many of us are utterly powerless in the face of the world's many problems. I get that. Some of us are more powerless than others. But many of us are in temporary control of a tiny little piece of the planet.

This little piece may only be your body—no more. (Sadly, it is possible that it may even be less than your body if others or circumstances have control over it. This is a terrible situation. The only thing you may have control over, then, is your mind.)

Or it may be your body and a small space around you. It may be a slightly bigger slice of the planet, or if you are a powerful person, it may be a much bigger piece.

Whatever piece you have some control over, even if it is not for very long, you can try (which could mean "pretend") to be the host of that piece.

This is not something complicated. You can be polite to your guests when someone comes to your house, big or tiny. You can show them courtesy. If they behave stupidly, you don't throw them out; you extend generosity to them and overlook their behavior. Of course, this is true within reasonable limits. If your guest wants to douse your house with gasoline and light it up, you can firmly stop that. Being a host doesn't mean you behave like a complete idiot.

We can entertain and behave courteously for at least a short while while our guests are around. We have the ability to act like good hosts.

In the after-meh phase, when we are relaxed and reflective, we can adopt the attitude of a host. This means we act kindly and generously to those around us, overlooking their minor stupidities and annoyances. Remember, some people may think we are stupid, annoying, or irritating, and if they overlook our mistakes, then don't we appreciate that? We can extend this courtesy to others.

It's never going to happen, but I am going to daydream a little. If everyone decided to behave like a host, would we have crises, wars, chaos, or destruction? Think about it. It seems small and probably sounds boring, but if all the people in the world universally tried to behave like kind hosts, wouldn't we have more peace on Earth? More kindness? Fewer atrocities?

An alternative to being a host is to think of yourself as a good friend. If you and I can be friends to those around us, even to those who are not our friends, wouldn't we overlook their little (or not so little) foibles? We allow our friends to get away with stuff we wouldn't let others get away with.

Being friendly also feels nice. When we feel friendly, we are in the glow of positive nanny mental states. From here, we can be generous, kind, and helpful. Plus, the positive states bring us benefits too.

HOW TO PRETEND: BEING A HOST OR A FRIEND

Being a host and being a friend are not impossible goals. We can cultivate these states by simply assuming them. In practical terms, this could mean pretending or acting the part of a host or a friend. Even when you pretend, there are two types of pretending. One type is when you are boiling and seething or irritated on the inside while being nice on the outside. This is not the type I recommend.

I advise you to try the second type of pretending.

Pretend you are a good host or friend. Imagine that you are one. Ask yourself, "What would I feel if I were a good host or friend? How would I act?" And then act in that way. Sure, you are pretending, but this is still wishing others well, being kind, and thinking kindly.

The pretending helps you taste what it feels like. The positive states of friendship and being a willing host are available to us, whether we really feel it or pretend to feel it. A real feeling is one we think is real and feel deep inside. A pretend feeling is one we assume. A real feeling may be more intense, but a pretend feeling gives us a taste. A taste we can grow to appreciate and savor. In time, the "pretend" may become the "real."

When we are commanded by a troubling nanny mental state, we can meh it, reflect realistically in the after-meh phase, and let the problematic nanny mental state drop off. We then have the choice of assuming a more positive attitude.

Or if we are in a neutral mental state, we can decide to adopt a positive state.

We can tell ourselves, "I am going to be a friendly host to those around me." You can even do something that might seem ridiculous but isn't. Pick a time, say, Thursday from 10 a.m. to noon. You decide to be a host and a friend for these two hours. Two hours isn't that much. You might find yourself in such a good mood that you decide to increase this to three or four hours or for your whole life—who knows!

Or you may run into problems. Someone could rub you the wrong way. This is the perfect time for you to try the meh technique: You watch, you meh, you meh the assumptions, and then you quickly enter the after-meh period. You can continue being a good host once you have disposed of the unproductive state.

This will give you a taste of this way of being. As your appreciation of this state grows, you will find yourself leaning more and more into it.

I learned an aspect of this from the wonderful *Building a Life Worth Living* by Marsha M. Linehan. Dr. Linehan is the founder of dialectical behavior therapy (DBT). She presents a superb idea: "You can't think yourself into a new way of acting; you can only act yourself into new ways of thinking."

This is a genuinely fantastic thought! We can appreciate its fruits when we start behaving like generous hosts and friends. *Our thinking changes as we act with kindness to ourselves and others.* We feel better about ourselves. We feel a little more in control (the control to act kindly). Our thoughts become kinder and less troublesome. We feel happier and more content (hopefully). And as Dr. Linehan writes, we *act* ourselves into new ways of thinking.

USEFUL SKILL 10: HAVING A GOOD SENSE OF HUMOR

Nanny mental states are serious and gloomy. When you feel

disturbed, it is because you have a nanny mental state that is disturbed. And since this is the state "on top" of your mental stage, you feel bad.

An *I* wrapped in a negative nanny mental state can only see things in its way—the *I* way. *I* is concerned with whatever is bothering it. It is the only thing that it can do.

When we meh this state, we see through it and observe that it is not as important, inevitable, urgent, or meaningful as it claims to be.

Luckily for us, having a sense of humor is a pleasant, feel-good attribute that can help us when we feel weighed down by a particularly burdensome nanny mental state. A sense of humor helps us see through false assumptions. Here's one of my favorite jokes: A man is painting something at top speed. Someone asks him why. He says he doesn't want the paint to run out.[18]

Anytime you feel stressed and have to get something done or else all hell will break loose, you can get a good laugh out of this. You may need to work quickly, but what good will it do if you make a mistake and have to repeat the task? Working fast is not always the smartest thing to do—it may last longer in the long run.

Meh and after-meh can get a hefty dose of help from a good sense of humor. Humor is the antidote to seriousness. If you can laugh, you can shift out of a gloomy and glum nanny mental state. When you laugh, you end up in a laughing nanny mental state (as opposed to a serious one). You also feel better. When you are relieved of the burden, you can focus on more reasonable thoughts. This can help you move confidently through the meh and after-meh phases.

Life, as we all know, is not a bed of roses. I came across a quote online that I don't remember exactly. It went something like this: Dear Life, when I asked, "How bad can it get," I

---

18 Shah, Idries. *Special Illumination*. ISF Publishing. Kindle.

didn't really want to find out. Another amusing quote about our predicament is this one: It gets worse before it gets worse. While these are dark, bleak sayings, they are humorous (to me, at least). Any time you feel bummed, humor can bring a little cheer to your life. You might get a tiny bounce, which will help you implement the strategies discussed in this book.

Or when you feel life is unfair, how about this to lighten the moment: *Dear Life, I've finally understood that you are unfair, so can you please stop teaching me this lesson over and over again?*

If you think greed or selfishness is good, try this: Two business partners are talking, and one says to the other, "Don't worry, when I said we're bankrupt, I meant that we're *morally* bankrupt." We may notice a flash of recognition when we read this. It feels nice to have tons of money, so we think it is "only natural" to feel greedy for money. Of course, when we meh and after-meh, we can see the reality of greed. This joke can inject some humor into the system, helping our meh to loosen the grip of a greedy nanny mental state.

I don't want to belabor the point. Humor is the antifreeze for frozen, rigid, inflexible nanny mental states. It helps meh get the job done. If you can see the humor of the situation, you have already shifted partly out of an unhelpful nanny mental state, and that's a good start.

PART 5

TWO FINAL POINTS

BLANK MEH—NO PLACE FOR NANNY MENTAL STATES

We now come to the end of our journey together. I will present some final thoughts on an aspect of meh that is especially appealing to me. It may not be everyone's cup of tea. I am still going to put it out there. Perhaps it will click with some readers.

Being a blank slate for an extended time is difficult or impossible. You can't turn off thoughts. Some people think meditation is about having no thoughts, but this is an impossibility. We always or nearly always have some thoughts. However, it is possible to have fragments of time when we find ourselves between thoughts. We will focus on these fragments.

In my case, the fragments are tiny—minuscule. I am usually hopping from one nanny mental state to another. The goal of this book has been to help transform negative nanny mental states into positive ones. The way has been by watching these states, saying *meh* to them and their assumptions, getting a more realistic understanding of the situation in the after-meh, and landing on a more positive nanny mental state.

That's it. This is the whole point of this entire book.

Now I want to introduce another idea, a fairly reasonable one, in my opinion. I want you to decide for yourself if it makes sense.

In addition to replacing unhelpful mental states with more positive, helpful ones, meh—or the idea behind meh—has another use.

It is to remove the negative mental state and then stay there without reaching out for another thought or mental state.

In practical terms, this would mean that after you have meh-ed a nanny mental state, you don't do anything more. You remain in silence for as long as you can:

STEP 1: Nanny mental state X arises.

STEP 2: Watch it, noting any sensations, physical or mental, that you have.

STEP 3: Say *meh* (loudly or silently, depending on whether you are alone or in company).

STEP 4: Remain in silence without a nanny mental state—any nanny mental state.

STEP 5: Repeat steps 1 to 4 for a short while (a minute, two, five, ten, whatever works).

You will keep entering tiny pieces of time, probably a few seconds or a bit more, in which you will have nothing on the top of your mind. Your mind will be blank.

Why do this?

It is a bit like pushing a reset button on a gadget or turning it off and back on.

When you "blank" out nanny mental states, you are now in

a place, a mental space, in which nothing is there, even if it is for a brief period. The periods add up over the time you allot for this purpose.

We have seen that many nanny mental states are counterproductive—I've been calling them mental troubles. They are unnecessary headaches; they don't help the situation, and in many cases, they hurt the situation.

Getting a break from these nanny mental states, even for minutes, is a welcome relief.

Please note that I don't mean a few minutes of an *uninterrupted* break from mental states. You must keep reentering blank states at any time you set aside for this purpose, as shown in steps 1 to 5 above.

The other advantage is that when we are freed up from these nanny mental states—even for a short while—our brain can work in the background and provide us with a fresh perspective or a possible solution to any problems we might be dealing with. The reason is that while we remain attached to a disturbing or vexing nanny mental state, we are unlikely to see any perspective different from the one the nanny mental state presents to us.

Our *I* can only present the *I* point of view.

Enter blank meh, where we clean out nanny mental states and rest in blankness. It's like taking a vacation or walking to clear your head. You come back recharged and energized.

Another advantage is that it feels very peaceful. I don't mean to turn you into a blank-meh junkie, but this quiet break from the constant chatter of nanny mental states is very relaxing indeed.

It seems as if blank meh takes us to a mental "place" where we don't have anything to identify or name. It is only blankness or "nothing."

This might be a leap, but blank meh reminds me of *The*

Cloud of Unknowing, the mystical treatise from the fourteenth century. We don't know who wrote this book. I want to draw attention to a point made by Dr. Marsha M. Linehan in her book *Building a Life Worth Living*, where she describes "acceptance of oneself . . . and embracing change toward a better life." She emphasizes that this combination of both "change strategies" and "acceptance strategies" makes dialectical behavioral therapy (DBT) "unique." It is generally accepted that DBT is a very effective form of therapy.

I found Dr. Linehan's analysis of *The Cloud of Unknowing* fascinating. The anonymous writer of this book of mystical contemplation advises us to "go into the cloud of unknowing." Why would one want to do that? In Dr. Linehan's opinion, it is to get to God. I want to draw a parallel to the blank state in which our thoughts are absent.

So, what does one find in this cloud of unknowing? First, only "darkness." Dr. Linehan, a psychologist and Zen master, explains that this cloud is a place "of no words, of no experience, of nothing." Dr. Linehan writes one of my favorite sentences from her book: "It is going into the spiritual path and not experiencing anything, but not worrying, because this is the spiritual path."

It is not my place to comment on spiritual paths, but I think blank meh is a bit like the path of "not experiencing anything" that Dr. Linehan describes. Here, I rest away from thoughts and am in a place I can't figure out or know. It is not known to me. But I come out of this place cleared of annoying nanny mental states, refreshed and energetic.

And that, indeed, is something.

I occasionally turn to this nothing place when I am troubled by something or can't find a solution to some problem. At such times, I enter the blank meh state and stay there for a short while. I have found this method helpful in clearing up my mental stage, allowing useful ideas to emerge and helping me deal with whatever bothers me. It is not a magic bullet. But I find it helpful, as well as being restful and relaxing.

A FINAL WORD: WHAT IF WE DON'T MEH?—CAN MEH HELP US FIND CONTENTMENT, FULFILLMENT, AND PEACE?

Imagine a person with very long hair covering the eyes, the entire face, and the mouth.

Imagine this person saying, "It grew while I wasn't watching."

Nanny mental states are like that. They can grow and take over. They do so openly, in full view, but they grow unnoticed if we aren't watching.

There is nothing new in this book. The strategy of meh is nothing other than practicing the old advice that we shouldn't believe every thought that arises in our minds. We shouldn't accept any and every nanny mental state.

But, to do so, we have to watch, and then we have to disregard. Meh is the strategy of disregarding.

If we don't disregard negative states, we might find ourselves stuck with the mental equivalent of really long hair.

When we meh and ignore and refuse to be impressed by the unhelpful garbage that often appears in our minds, we open ourselves to many possibilities. We have seen that when the negative nanny mental states drop off, we open ourselves to other states, states in which we are not troubled, bored, dissatisfied, irritated, upset, dispirited, despairing, angry, wrathful, and seething with negative emotions. You could say that we find ourselves in a happier place, where we are not running after this or that. In a word, we are content.

We could then end up in mental states where we might see facets of situations hidden from us, helping us find creative solutions to problems, where we can do more with less tension.

Once we get past the negative nanny mental state, we enter a mental place or space where we may find that thing we call fulfillment. What is fulfillment? Fulfillment, in one sense, is reaching our potential—whatever state is possible to us, given our circumstances. With the power of meh, we have seen how we can cast aside the negative and embrace the positive. We can become kinder, helpful, supportive, happier beings. We can help each other. We can help ourselves. We can end our obsession with ourselves, our demands, and our wants (disguised as needs). We can't stop what's coming to us, but at least we can feel more at peace.

And what about world peace? Can you imagine what would happen if people universally became kinder to each other? Wouldn't we have world peace? Sadly, I don't foresee that happening anytime soon, so don't hold your breath. But we can bring peace to the "world" inside us, to our minds. We can bring peace to the tiny corner we have some temporary control over. That's about all we can do. Good luck to all of us! Happy meh-ing!

ACKNOWLEDGMENT

I am very grateful to Megan Ketcham, who used the phrase "the power of meh" and inspired me to write this book.

www.ingramcontent.com/pod-product-compliance
Lightning Source LLC
LaVergne TN
LVHW091543070526
838199LV00002B/188